Turning Points

A Memoir Anthology

Evergreen Writers

Cover art: Carolyn Campbell

Organizing Committee: Carolyn Campbell, Peggy Markham, Kay Crook, Marcia Jones, Connie Bierkan, and Jean Bell

"Turning Points: A Memoir Anthology," by Evergreen Writers. ISBN 978-1-62137-914-0 (hardcover); 978-1-62137-913-3 (softcover). Published 2016 by Virtualbookworm.com Publishing, P.O. Box 9949, College Station, TX , 77842, US.

INTRODUCTION

Everyone has a story, a lifetime of memories to preserve or share with family and friends. The smallest memory holds fascination for someone. As technology changes the way things used to be, small towns disappear, rural communities and farms give way to urban neighborhoods, and friends and family come and go, it is vital to record our point in time.

Memoir as creative writing is a way to tell our own story and invites others to share the experience. Sometimes, we write about a piece of nostalgia, a family tradition, overcoming an illness, remembering World War II, growing up in the American South or on a farm in the Midwest. Sometimes we describe an important person in our lives, a travel experience or immigrating to America.

As a memoir teacher for the past twenty years, I've had the privilege of sharing countless stories – sad, happy, funny, or inspirational. The writers are on a journey; some are beginners, while others are more experienced; some have published their work or received recognition in awards.

The memoirs in this anthology are written to be read and they are true.

Carolyn Evans Campbell

Contents

Lynn Allbright

THE PURPLE CHAIR

Past the false statuary and uniformly manicured yards of my mother-in-law's neighborhood, I escape into the collage of the alley. Even though she will find and chastise my collecting, I gather some interesting discards. My love of the work of the Post War Expressionists makes the world seem less presumptuous. Ahead sits a massive purple velvet chair crested with orange lichen, a sight that would drop any artist to her knees. I don't miss the mania of balancing painting and family.

"You didn't cut through anyone's yard?"

"No." (I'm 62.)

"What'd you see anyway?"

"I saw an idea."

BUS TRIP TO SAN BLAS

On the shoulder of the Periferico, just past the small pyramid sprinkled with obsidian, we wait in the glittering March sunlight for the bus to San Blas. The village peasants watch us choose a seat behind the woman with shiny black hair pinned in an infinity twist. She clutches an iridescent rooster to her chest and is wrapped in a colorful striped fabric. I look out the front of the bus. A strip of red pompoms across the top of the windshield bops to a transistor radio playing Mariachi music. Smiles in the rear view mirror flash gold teeth and the mood is happy.

In the middle of a large number of passengers at the next stop a vendor hops on board. He is selling thick potato chips covered in coarse salt and paprika. We purchase a bag and the man squeezes fresh lime juice over the warm crisp slices. We share a bottle of Modelo and I lean back against your shoulder. I have a feeling you know what you are doing.

THE NECESSARY PLACE

The ravine was a deep cleave in the forest floor perpendicular to the main upper trail. We had never been able to find where it fanned out in a delta and into the Critchel Gulch below. A dozen or more ravines were traversable on horseback and each held a unique wonderland of flora and fauna. But this one with its enormous depth and steep banks seemed navigable only by eye.

It was the last unexplored territory in the middle of thousands of acres, an unspoken dare. We dismounted at the half-buried tractor tire which served as a marker or corner stone and looked over the lush green mosses, and the gray, orange, white and black lichens with their tiny trumpets bursting. The growth carpeted rock, stumps and fallen trees. Fir, spruce, pine, Ginella Maple and River Birch sprouts stippled the walls of the huge gouge in the earth. A canopy of taller trees puttered in the wind. Colored grass tassels ran in waves up the steep banks, and the oldest tree tottered on the ravine's pebbled edge. Soaring in height, they created a sense of vertigo and astonishment in the onlooker, like rocketing exclamation points.

Monkshood, Shooting Star and violets spackled the black, musky, sweet-smelling earth. Our nostrils flared involuntarily. On the other side we saw the afternoon sun cut into little dancing fragments by the arms and legs of the foliage. A cathedral window stood shimmering in the woods. The beauty and magic of this place moved us. We tied up the horses and descended into the dark green.

Crab-walking feet first, we saw the bottom come into view. Stark white calligraphy, next a grin of white piano key shapes, running leg configurations, vertebral alignments, and hooves. Dozens and dozens of them. Hooves with shoes.

Paula Bard

BACK FROM THE WAR

Ears cocked, he traveled like a hungry cat. Focused. His prowling shadow loomed up the dark buildings as he stealthily moved through city streets. His heart yearned for the sound, melodies resonating through brick and concrete.

Faint strains of *Lazy River* curled around the tall brick buildings, and threads of clarinet were tempting, beckoning. Somewhere, this dark city concealed the treasure of his beloved instrument. The sweet sounds bounced and echoed, its essence distilled, pure.

This lone clarinet, now on to *Somebody Stole My Gal*, spoke to him; this was his music. Jazz. Taunting. Calling in this night-hushed city. His instrument, the soulful clarinet played with such passion. Such precision. The hunter moved closer and closer to the night's lone musician.

Who could this be, he wondered, in Midtown late on a Thursday night, theaters just out, night owls jostling toward clubs, dance halls, taxis racing, honking? New York City, still at this hour crazy awake, alive.

No longer a war-weary soldier haunting the streets of Paris or Morocco at the war's end, sniffing jazz out around every corner, he was home now, in New York City; a city pulsing with jazz, truly American music that had pierced his heart and laid claim.

Just up ahead, in the middle of the next block, that insistent clarinet lifted up and out of a basement club, intertwined with enthusiastic clapping. A tattered green awning, *Joe's*, long ago etched into the fabric, welcomed him as he headed down the dark stairs into the hot, packed, subterranean world of old beer, whiskey, and sharp cigarette smoke – while the sweetest music he had ever heard danced up those dark stairs, filling the street and bouncing lightly off the dour facades of hulking brick buildings.

There he was, on the back stage, a sole clarinet player, wailing away on a beautiful black clarinet. Yes, it was him! Dark hair, glasses, the King of Swing, icon of the era, was just finishing up his set and now setting his clarinet down on its delicate metal stand, shaking hands as he made his way up to the bar in the front of the smoky room.

They smiled and shook hands, this just reluctantly-returned-home soldier and Benny Goodman, and in that moment, the love of jazz grabbed my father's soul and brought him home from the war.

SWEETS OF CHILDHOOD

Shelves tower over my head: two long aisles crammed with Kellogg's Corn Flakes, Shredded Wheat boxes, Campbell's Tomato Soup cans and peanut butter jars, foods, detergents, aspirin, and band-aids. It is dim, always dim – no windows. At the end of the isle, brooms are propped together like stalks of wheat, stiff bristles pointing straight up. Years of cleaning with ammonia and racks of produce near the front door interlace with a slightly damp and pungent air.

Dominating the center of the room is a big meat case, silver and white metal with a thick nicked glass face. Through the glass, I can see several big, flesh-colored lumps of raw meat and a steel slicing machine. I am never tall enough to see over the top, but can always hear a bellowing voice. I was pretty sure that there was a large, red-faced man back there with a blood-spattered white apron, clattering away. "What'll ya have Mrs. Jackson, fine cut of beef brisket? Just cook 'er up slowly with some onion, potatoes, and rosemary, voilà dinner fit for a king!" I always edged carefully back toward the front of the store.

I recall a small, dingy, white house connected behind the store where the owners lived. *Did he eat dinner in that blood-stained apron?* I could just imagine the family dinner table, gathered around big slabs of roasted meat and booming voices, "Pass the roast beef, Marge!"

Oh yes, he was to be avoided!

Sargent's Market was our destination after ballet class on Thursday afternoons. Kathy Bresee, my fellow dancer, tall and angular, on-and-off-best friend, walked to the corner of Spruce and Ford from downtown, when we were speaking.

But, what we were after when we arrived, tired from dancing on those light-faded Thursday afternoons, was the big glass case at the front of the store. A sumptuous case of desire: rows of Juicy Fruit; Black Jack; Double Mint *double your fun* gum; Sugar Babies in yellow and red bags – too sweet; Zero Bars; Almond Joys; Sweet Tarts; Butterfingers; black, white, and pink boxes of licorice Good and

Plenty, perfect for shaking. Oh, to our ten-year-old eyes these were the temptations of paradise!

"Okay girls, what'll it be, this time, Reese's Peanut Butter Cups? How 'bout some Tootsie Roll Pops?" The sales girl eyes us carefully, raises her eyebrows, waits impatiently. After much deliberation, we always bought one piece of candy each; something sweet for that final leg home. Then we split, each to make her own way. I always tried to make my candy last those last four blocks, trudging up the hill on slate sidewalks, under gracious maple tree tents, and between overgrown, slipping stone walls, to 18 Central Avenue and dinner.

In the summer, we mostly biked all over town, and it was Sargent's frozen case that beckoned, almost too cold to reach into, full of soft and chocolatey ice cream sandwiches and Fudgsicles, a chocolatey mess running down bicycle fingers. My favorite discovery was luscious, orange ice cream over vanilla on-a-stick, Creamsicles. Heaven!

Our small town of Oneonta, New York was dotted with small, family grocery stores. Bob's was three blocks in the other direction. In late summer, green tasseled ears tumbled out of faded wicker baskets in front of the store; *best sweet corn in the Catskills.* Except for that sweet corn, my mother never shopped for our family in those little grocery stores. She drove to the big new Victory Market downtown with its wide aisles, fluorescent lights, and huge parking lot across from the stone-grey Methodist church.

But these little grocery store gems were the secret destination of kids all over town. We never told our parents, in those years before first jobs. Most likely, the money used was not given graciously, or even knowingly, so best not to divulge our secrets!

But, of course, best to have secrets!

Jean Barringer

LEAVING MY COUNTRY

I walked out onto the tarmac with my four-month-old baby in my arms. The airplane that was to carry us to Canada stood waiting, and it didn't look big enough to be flying such a distance. "A Constellation," they told me, not even a super Constellation which was a larger model of the same plane. It was 6 PM on a dark cold evening, March 2, 1954, and I was traveling alone, my husband having gone ahead of me a month earlier. This was my very first flight.

I wasn't nervous, but very excited, it was an adventure. The flight attendant took us on ahead of the other passengers because of the baby, up the metal staircase and onto the aircraft. I was seated at the rear of the plane along with a young couple who also had a baby. There weren't many other passengers, I remember. I suppose it wasn't the best time of year to be flying to Canada, but it didn't occur to me that it was still winter, and there could be weather issues. I didn't think about it.

The other passengers boarded, the doors closed, and the captain announced that our first stop for refueling would be Keflavik, Iceland. I looked out at the lighted terminal buildings of Prestwick Airport, situated west of Glasgow on the west coast of Scotland. We trundled out onto the runway and turned around at the far end. One by one the four engines were tested, and then very slowly the plane moved down the runway, gathering speed as it went. I saw the lights of the airport as we passed them, and then they were gone.

I felt the aircraft lift into the air and kind of hesitate for a moment before the engines took us through the clouds into a starlit sky. I wished it had been daylight so that I could see where we were. I knew we would be passing over the beautiful Western Isles, the

Inner and Outer Hebrides, on the way to Iceland, but all I could see were the stars and the wing with the lights flashing on the end.

After a couple of hours we began to descend, and I could see the lights below. Keflavik had been an American airbase during World War II, and we were told we would be landing and that all passengers would be required to disembark while we refueled, all except the babies; and the stewardess would remain on board to care for them. I didn't much care for that idea, but that's how it was.

As we all went down the staircase to the tarmac, we were met by the most intense cold I had ever encountered. Snow was blowing across the tarmac in a ground blizzard, and I was glad then that I wasn't carrying Christopher through that wind and cold. The airport building was a Quonset hut, the remnant of the old airbase – a large bare hut with trestle tables and benches, but warm and welcoming. They gave us hot chocolate and cookies while we waited. On the walls around us were torn posters; photographs of pin-up girls like Betty Grable, Dorothy Lamour, and Lana Turner; and boards with signatures of the airmen who only a few years ago were based there. Crews of the air-rescue planes, Cansos, or PBYs that flew out over the North Atlantic, patrolling the convoys, ever watchful for the U-boats on the prowl. It was a strange spooky feeling to be there, full of the ghosts of the young men who had called Keflavik home during World War II.

After a while we were called to re-board, and once again, the engines were started, taking time to warm up in that cold air. All four propellers were tested one after another, and we took off and headed west.

The baby was fine all this time tucked up in his little cocoon of blankets. I fed him and he slept again. I didn't sleep at all, I sat and watched the stars as they rocked up and down, up and down.

How would it be in Canada? I was going first to Montreal where I would be staying with friends for a week before traveling on to Toronto. Anthony was already working as a field-geologist in Northern Ontario and would be flown out by bush plane in order to meet me and get me settled before returning to the bush.

I must have slept because it was sometime later that I felt the plane bank and swing to the South. Once more we were to land to refuel, this time in Gander, Newfoundland, and as the headlights switched on I could see the snow blowing past. We landed on a very bumpy runway. I don't think it could have been used very much in 1954. The lights showed a few hangars and huts; this was the airport then.

We were allowed to take the babies with us this time, and made our way through a canyon of snow towering way above our heads. The airport workers wore parkas with fur-lined hoods and bright checked jackets and hats with ear flaps. Canadians looked so very different from Brits. I realized that neither of us had clothes that were suitable for that cold climate. It would have to be my first priority.

Inside the warm hut we were given hot coffee and ham sandwiches, and I was able to get some warm water to make Christopher's formula; then we were back on the airplane and on our way to Montreal.

Still another four hours to go, but it turned into five hours and then five and a half as we circled Montreal in a blizzard. Finally at 6 AM we landed, and I carried my screaming baby through the snow. There was immigration to go through and baggage to claim, and then I found – nobody to meet me!

The people at Trans-Canada Airlines, as it was then, were kindness itself; they took care of everything. They gave me a private room to sit in while I changed and fed the baby, gave me hot tea and scrambled eggs, and then phoned my friend, Eileen, to say I had arrived. I had not thought that, of course, she couldn't meet me at 6 AM. She also had a young child and no car. And so it was that TCA got me a taxi and sent me on my way.

As we drove out onto the highway, we had to stop at a railroad crossing while the biggest locomotive I had ever seen came slowly by, bell clanging, snowplow on the front, and Canadian Pacific in large letters on the side. This giant train went by, I'm sure for my benefit, many huge cars, and finally a caboose. It couldn't have been a more fitting introduction to the country I had come to.

My friends' apartment was modest, but comfortable. Outside the temperature was down near zero, but that little apartment was so warm. I keep mentioning that word "warm," and I think that the warmth of the buildings I went into is what impressed me more than anything else. I had come from a country where houses were so cold inside – one small fireplace heated one room, the rest of the house ice cold. In fact, there were icicles hanging from the bathroom faucets all winter. Everybody suffered from chilblains, a form of frostbite. Fingers and toes became red and swollen, itched and burned, then broke and bled. I remember not being able to hold a pencil at school, my fingers were so swollen. There in Montreal, in that glorious *warmth*, my swollen chilblains disappeared in a few days.

Eileen took me to a supermarket. We didn't have supermarkets in Britain at that time, and I simply stood in the doorway and stared in amazement at all the food on display. In Britain food was still rationed in 1954. I don't remember ever having seen this amount of food: long display cases of meat, cut and packaged, eggs, butter and cheese, bottles of milk in refrigerators, and shelves packed with tea and coffee, jams and canned fruit. The displays of fruit and vegetables astounded me – I couldn't take it all in, there was so much!

These people, these Canadians looked so different from the people I had left behind. They had color in their cheeks, the children were round and healthy, the young people tall, muscular, and bright-eyed. How different it all was! But it was the happy laughter that I remember most. Canadians had jobs, and owned their homes with their own kitchens and bathrooms. They didn't have to share. They had refrigerators and washing machines, some had dryers even, and a lot of them had cars. They didn't know about, or understand, what life was like in Europe. How could they possibly understand?

I knew then that I was ready to live in this happy country, adopt new ways, and accept whatever life had in store for me. But life, as I was about to find out, had a great many obstacles lying in wait for me.

A week later, a taxi took Christopher and me to the airport for the flight to Toronto. We boarded a *North Star*, which turned out to be a rickety old aircraft left over from goodness knows when, but I was much too interested in the landscape I was flying over to notice the bumps. We flew along the St. Lawrence River, still ice bound, across the rolling snow-covered border country of Southern Ontario with small towns dotting the countryside, across the shores of Lake Ontario, and finally over the massed buildings of Toronto.

In 1954, Toronto was not the huge prosperous city it is now, and the airport was a few hangars and two little Quonset huts. Amazing when I think of the giant terminal buildings there now. The plane landed on a bumpy runway and rolled to a stop. I could see the two huts and some cars parked on a small unpaved parking lot. Where was Anthony? I suddenly had horrible misgivings that he wouldn't be there – maybe he was held up in the bush because of weather.

I was last off the plane and helped by the stewardess. I made my way across the snow packed ground, and there he was. A fellow geologist had driven him to meet me, and he looked every inch a Canadian in a red and black checked coat and a hat with fur ear flaps.

Thinking back now, I realize that I had come to a town, hardly a city, still part of a very rural landscape, but beginning to push out to the north, east, and west. What a different lifestyle this was going to be, but I was ready and eager to open the door and step into a new world.

THE WAY THINGS WERE

Pat McKenzie's hardware store stood in the High Street facing the bank on the opposite side of the street.

Forres was a market town. Farmers came to town and visited the hardware store for all their agricultural needs. It was a very busy place.

Granny would send me on errands, and I loved going to Pat McKenzie's hardware store for her kitchen candles, bar soap for laundry, and clothes pegs.

Over the years Mr. McKenzie was joined by Mr. Cruickshank, and the name over the door was repainted in gold on green, *McKenzie and Cruickshank.* It was still the same fascinating store, smelling pungently of creosote and old rope. The floorboards still creaked, and they still sold nuts and bolts and screws; little brass hooks and hasps; hammers and saws and screwdrivers of all shapes and sizes.

Mr. McKenzie was tall and broad and bristled with a curly red beard, eyebrows that stuck out over twinkly blue eyes, while Mr. Cruickshank was short and dumpy and bald. He wore steel framed glasses and had jowls that wobbled when he spoke or laughed.

Both gentlemen wore brown aprons with large capacious pockets, each divided into smaller, narrower pockets out of which protruded wooden folding rulers, scissors, and notebooks. Each of them had pencils lodged behind their ears, as carpenters do, and both gentlemen knew how to fix everything.

In my grandmother's day we all went to bed by candlelight, so the hardware store was well stocked with oil lamps embellished with roses and violets and of course lamp oil, fancy chamber pots, and candlestick holders with handles on the sides and saucers to catch the wax.

They sold bellows to hang by the fireplace. On the wall, hung washboards and below them trays of Sunlight Soap. There were sticks for lifting hot laundry out of the copper pot to put through the mangle. They sold mangles too and flat irons and trivets. All kinds of necessary items came from McKenzie and Cruickshank's Hardware Store, and I loved going in and smelling the *hardware-y* smells.

Farmers gathered there on market day to discuss the weather and the state of the crops that year, all of them weather-beaten with windburned faces and big Scottish noses. All Scotsmen seem to have big noses.

Other farmers kept sheep or cattle, and all had border collies to help bring the livestock down from the hills. All the dogs had fleas and scratched themselves constantly.

Market day was particularly busy for the farmers. They were everywhere on the High Street bringing their wives, who did their shopping and met other wives and stood in groups gossiping.

Those were lovely days, but after World War II things changed. My sister tells me *McKenzie and Cruickshank* is still there, though Mr. McKenzie and Mr. Cruickshank are long gone. The oil lamps are gone, too. So are the candlesticks and kitchen candles. Nobody washes on a washboard now or uses Sunlight Soap.

Electric devices have replaced oil lamps, and it's a different, less interesting store. You can still buy gardening tools, and there is a pervasive smell of fertilizers sold in big plastic bags. A lot of *gift-y things* for sale, but the floor boards still creak "although they are replacing them with vinyl squares," my sister says.

When I came to Evergreen forty years ago I was astonished to find the same hardware store I left behind in Scotland, also smelling of creosote and old rope. You could buy one screw if you wanted, and it would be put into the same little brown paper bag. It also had the same creaky floor boards and wooden staircase. It was one of my favorite places to go.

Sad, sad when it closed. Didn't they realize what a gold mine they had? I know things change, sometimes for the better, sometime not. But I think it's important for us who remember to write it down so that those who come after will know the way things were.

Jean Bell

HITTING A POLICE CAR

I was in no condition to be driving that hot summer evening in 1974. I was already in tears before the cop pulled me over, red and blue lights flashing, sirens blaring, on the sloping exit from the long bridge over the Schuylkill River. As he approached my car, I was a mess – too flustered to roll my window down, then couldn't find my driver's license or car registration.

Newly divorced, that day I'd come back to meet my ex-husband at our home – now his – to collect my things and divvy up the few possessions we had acquired in common. He got the furniture, all vintage garage sale, since I was the one moving two thousand miles away to start a new life in the wide open spaces of the American West. I got the stereo, he the television, and we haggled for hours over our mutual love of music in the form of treasured LP albums. In the end we took turns: I picked a Cat Stevens album, he picked the Beatles *Yellow Submarine*, and so it went, slowly and dismally, through the entire collection.

Exhausted, I started loading my belongings into my car, but when I picked up the first speaker he wouldn't let me take it. The speakers were furniture he insisted, not part of the stereo. Furious beyond the replacement cost of the speakers, I exploded. How like him to nitpick about speakers when he got the house, the furniture, his new lover, and I got stuck with a broken heart and whatever I could fit in the back of an old Fiat.

I briefly considered dividing the speakers, one for him and one for me, the way we divvied up the records. But it would have killed the matched set. So, like the mother in the Bible story of King Solomon's judgment, I offered to give them both up rather than ruin the pair. Unfortunately, King Solomon wasn't there to come to my rescue. I finished packing my remaining stuff and drove madly away from the house, my heart and pride damaged almost beyond repair.

When the cop who had pulled me over gruffly ordered me to get out of the car, I obeyed. However, I forgot to set the parking brake. He and I watched in horror as my car rolled back into his police cruiser. Suddenly more police cars materialized as if waiting in the next block for the cop's call and my bad behavior. To my relief, when they saw the damage confined to a small dent in my own bumper they disappeared as quickly as they'd come.

Standing bereft by the side of the road in my paisley miniskirt, I couldn't hold myself together any longer and began to sob uncontrollably. The officer realized his biggest problem was not a traffic ticket, it was a hysterical young woman. Changing his tack, he spoke in soft soothing tones and gradually calmed me to the level of quiet hiccups.

He gave me a ticket for the alleged original offense of going through a red light a mile before the bridge. And another ticket for driving without a license. Then he let me go with an additional warning about setting my brakes.

Looking back from the vantage of forty years, I can laugh at the scene of the crime, at the insult of a petty argument over speakers, even at the divorce. Now that I think about it, hitting a police car was a lot like how my marriage disintegrated – through unintended neglect.

PLAYING A METAPHOR

We're just finishing lunch when my grandson, age twenty-two months, notices the ice scraper lying near the door on its way out to the car the first snowy day of winter. He toddles over, picks it up, climbs onto a chair, puts the scraper on his lap and starts playing with it: one small hand on its long handle, one hand moving repeatedly across the fat end of the brush.

His mom and I watch, mystified, since he doesn't yet have enough language to tell us what he's doing. But he looks up at us expectantly.

His mom finally realizes he's holding the ice scraper like his babysitter plays her guitar! Mom and I sing "Row, row, row your boat ..." while Shinji plays on and beams his happiness that we get the joke.

Whoever says you need to know how to talk before you can have fun with words never saw a mime at work, or a toddler playing a tune on an ice scraper.

Kathi Bernier

DEAD AUNTS

A dining room table floats to the top of memory like a printed fortune in a smoky crystal ball. The room is shrouded with velvet drapes, windows shaded by polished leaves guarded by gardenia bushes against the heat of Sunday afternoon.

Aunt Jeanie was as layered as an artichoke with tender parts at the end of dry leaves. She bore six children in the attempt to produce Tom the III. Born again at forty, she ran off with a twenty-year-old Christian folk singer, returning ten years later to play guitar while her children and grandchildren sang, "There are no flies on Jesus."

Aunt Suzanne was a goulash of unexpected spices. Hungarian, she was a fair copy of the Gabors, permed blonde hair, big white smile, and Max Factor skin. Her kindness floated in a cloud of Chanel Number Five. She won the Great Pierced Ears debate, giving me my first earrings. She startled us all one Easter by falling to the floor and speaking in tongues just before dessert.

Aunt Colleen was yogurt and black strap molasses — tart and unexpectedly sticky — a hippie thirty years too early. She tried to stay a tomboy, faithfully applying a rolling pin to her persistent breasts. She called it the Junior Bump Control. When we went to Mardi Gras, she refused to wear white gloves at the balls and ran off to the jazz joints in the French Quarter.

Aunt Gayle was champagne, bubbling and fizzing through every meal — a grown up Shirley Temple singing at the drop of a fork. Once she found an egg left from last year's hunt, broke it laughing at the cloud of dust. Her husband and kids joined the Mormon Church where she gave a famous drunken monologue. She died with purple veins mapping her legs, her liver hardened.

Aunt Cynthia was the cake left out in the rain, her melted face iced with bright makeup. She came from Las Vegas and lived in a white Frank Lloyd Wright house in the hills. The floors were covered with polar bear rugs. Large, dusty birds of prey hung from the ceilings. Cynthia was a skinny Mae West, a tin foil caricature covering genuine gold.

The table is cleared now. The dishes washed and put away somewhere in California. The house is now in black Beverly Hills. I think Nat King Cole's granddaughter lives there.

Connie Bierkan

ROCK-A-BYE BABY

It was December 26th, 1951, six weeks before Mama's due date. An orange sun crested the horizon where farms, not yet awakened by crowing roosters or lowing cattle lay blanketed by five inches of freshly fallen snow. Mama, Papa, and Gramma were all sneaking out of town. It was a pitiful sight to see three grown-ups tiptoeing around the car in dawn's lengthening shadows. I ought to know. I was there. Though I wasn't born yet.

Mama flung the rear passenger door open and plunked herself heavily into the back seat of his car. It jostled me inside her womb and, knowing me, I probably kicked in protest. I heard the man-person bark, "Hey, watch it! You almost took the door off its hinges."

"Well, I didn't, so quit your complainin'."

"Just wanted to help..."

"I'd have asked if I wanted it."

The car was a brand new '52 four-door Chevy Deluxe Bel Air, a gift the man's father had given him as a graduation present from college. A top-of-the-line hardtop coupe, screaming *look at me,* I bet Mama neither cared for the two-tone paint job, nor any of the other flashy accessories it boasted such as the white-walled tires.

"It's a bit over the top if you ask me. But then nobody's askin' so I guess I'll keep my mouth shut," Mama snorted as she slid across the leather-upholstered seat. Apparently, standard cloth was too ordinary for her college-graduate-ex-honey, but she had to concede the leather did smell pretty good – even in her delicate condition. I kinda liked it, too.

"Good idea, Missy, about keepin' your trap shut," warned Gramma. "I'll hear no nonsense today."

Mama sat and stared out the split glass windshield deliberately ignoring how her once-upon-a-time-beau, lover, soon-to-be-ex, father-of-her-child fussed over her mother. His ceremoniously getting Gramma settled in the front seat, tucking her heavy woolen skirt and coat in and around her, gently shutting the heavy door with a soft thud and then loading the suitcases into the trunk were all simply a means to avoid eye contact with Mama. So, my mother made sure she was in his direct line of sight in the rear view mirror. There, she could smirk and make him as uncomfortable as possible throughout the journey. Even if it made her uncomfortable. Personally? I was all for it!

Gramma stared straight ahead, too. Knees pressed tightly together under wintertime layers and lips pursed, she no doubt clutched a small pocketbook with both gloved hands. Mother and daughter, one in the front and one in the back, both clenched their teeth, neither uttering a word. I kept quiet, too.

A drowsy sort of snowfall dappled the windows while rays of sunshine reached into the interior to glint off the metal dashboard. Dust motes swirled in that bright beam, creating an evangelical tableau of righteousness inside the car where Mama, pregnant and unmarried, was spotlighted as an unrepentant sinner. Looming over the two eyes of the split windshield an awning, looking every bit like a giant uni-eyebrow, gave the car's countenance the same scowling expression as Mama's. *Typical*, she thought, *this after-market awning option is all about making a statement. Dumb. What did I ever see in this show-off?*

"He's got dollars, but not much sense," she muttered to me as he climbed behind the steering wheel. With a backward glance at Mama, he reversed too aggressively out the snow-packed driveway. Mama grabbed the hand rail and glowered at him in the mirror. I could feel her bracing her feet in order to better balance me in her womb. I didn't complain.

In those days it probably took four hours to make the journey to Chicago as Eisenhower's federal highway system had yet to be built. On two-lane roads through farming villages and small towns of no more than a few hundred in population, the trip was made all the more painfully slow by the absurd silence within the Chevy. It echoed miserably to the snowy stillness outside. Fields of cows and sheep were becoming fewer and fewer as we neared the Windy City, Chicago's apt nickname. Farms, most of them in tidy shape, boasted tractors idled by the winter season sitting out front under feet of snow. Studded sheet-metal silos bursting with stored grain were a testament to the success and/or wealth of a farmer by how many he had out back. They glinted in the white glare of sun on snow. Red barns and loafing sheds dotted the landscape, too. These were Mama's favorites because the earthiness spoke to her as it would me, too, when I grew up.

What was most curious, though, was how man-made boundaries disappeared under the deep snow. Fences, which usually made for dependable distinctions between what's yours and what's mine, just simply disappeared. It was a reminder that not too much faith could be put in such artificial delineations. Mama had always believed that with fences you actually had more freedom, that you knew your place or where you belonged. In a vacuum where everything is erased with white you don't know where you are. You are trapped by the endless expanse of being neither here nor there.

Occasionally, though, a small Currier & Ives town would surprise Mama along the way. I could tell because she'd lean her forehead against the frosted window and sigh with a sad longing as she looked into one charming house after another. Picket fences festooned with boughs of fir, front porches decked with garlands of holly, mistletoe swaying above so many front doors were all testaments of hope and joy. There would be families inside gathered around Christmas trees enjoying the aftermath of her most favorite holiday, one her family could ill afford. Folks enjoying leftovers of turkey sandwiches jammed with white meat, cranberry sauce, lettuce and mayo; a fistful of Lay's potato chips on the side and a cold glass of fresh cow's milk to wash it down. She imagined children playing on brightly colored braided rugs with toys delivered by Santa Claus, moms and dads reading the Saturday Evening Post while a fire crackled in the grate. She undoubtedly envisioned puppies or kittens tumbling in discarded wrapping paper and ribbons... All along the way she watched idyllic Norman Rockwell moments unfold. I knew she was thinking, *That's s'posed to be me in there...*

Big tears slid down her cheeks, hanging first from her nose and then her chin. And as each mile of road propelled her unwillingly closer to the city where our lives were about to be altered forever, I felt her sagging posture kneading me into a pretzel. With unblinking eyes forward as if in a trance, and with only the slightest movement of her hand back and forth, she caressed her rounded midriff. I surely was grateful for the affection and hoped I could transmit it back to her.

Even though he was at the wheel, she'd already said goodbye to the man who had promised to marry and keep her always. That happened weeks earlier when he flat out refused to marry her. Said his parents could never abide a shotgun wedding and besides, wives were supposed to be virgins. But parting with the baby she'd kept safe and who'd kept her warm these past seven months? Me, in other words? That would be a test she couldn't fathom enduring. Me neither.

As we entered the outskirts of Chicago from the south side, Mama couldn't bear the silence any more.

"Would it be too much to ask for the radio to be turned on?" Gramma looked over her shoulder at Mama in the back seat with a frown of rebuke while Mama shrugged her shoulders. Chicago's outskirts were an endless set of junk yards with boring spans of chain-link fencing. Parallel railroad tracks crowded with sooty boxcars full of coal and suffering livestock were depressing. Factory smokestacks spewing thick chemical fumes and stockyards filled with cargo containers foretold a cold reality. Mama tensed. Even frozen Lake Michigan, sparkling under a spray of snowflakes like a vision in a snow cone, couldn't engage her. There was no hope in that landscape, just an ominous chill spreading as far as the eye could see. Skyscrapers looming ahead made her feel very small as the city streets morphed into towering cement canyons. A grey landscape of steel, concrete, grey stone and grey mortar confronted them. With hoarfrost spreading its sheet of icy grey across their path, even the men and women walking briskly to and fro were grey in countenance and dress. So, too, drifts of slush. Grey. This urban jungle would be home for the next six weeks, and Mama was feeling queasy. Adding to her misery, she thought if she coughed or sneezed, she might wet her underpants.

"Are we there yet?" she asked petulantly. "It may surprise one of you that a girl in my condition needs to visit the john more than once on a six-hour road trip."

"Almost there," he said. "Sit tight." And with that he turned the radio on.

Mike Wallace's familiar voice invaded our space with the top-of-the-hour news. The impending expiration to the Marshall Plan being the headline, all three of the grown-ups listened. Unable to fathom what $13.3 billion dollars even looked like, Mama, I could tell, yawned with the tedium of it all. She seemed annoyed, nonetheless, by all that money going toward rebuilding Europe and not America after the war. *Who's gonna rebuild Pearl Harbor?* she thought. *Didn't our boys die saving them from annihilation? They should be paying us!* Next was a story about Libya becoming independent from Italy. *So what?* Finally, this: a sailor in Sweden is fined for kissing in public and the court calls his actions "obnoxious behavior repulsive to the public moral." At that Mama rolled her eyes and caught Papa's eye in the rearview mirror. *Wow, good thing you don't live in Sweden. Your sorry ass would be in jail!* The station was quickly changed. Soft strains of Perry Como's hit, *If,* filled the car with its sentimental lyrics:

If they made me king
I'd be but a slave to you
If I had everything
I'd still be a slave to you
If I ruled the night
Stars and moon so bright...

"Enough of that!" Gramma barked as she snapped the radio off. "That gobbledygook is what got you two idiots into trouble in the first place."

Even I, inside Mama's womb, could feel her anger as it radiated all the way into the back seat where we were stretched out across the bench. Today, when I think about the Gramma I'd never meet, I don't blame her, really. How mortified she must have been by

Mama's condition. It was so taboo. And since Mr. Spermatozoid was refusing to marry Mama, claiming he had a fiancée waiting back home, I imagine it was all she could do to get my mama away from home as quickly as possible. Escorting her daughter to a Home for Unwed Mothers would have been the last thing she'd ever have imagined doing. Worse, the very man who'd gotten Mama pregnant was doing the driving. He'd insisted!

You know, there's something wrong with that. Here he abandons my mama, and me for that matter, but wants to escort her to Illinois. Why? To make sure she goes through with the whole adoption business? Because he doesn't trust her? Because she might run away and hit him up later for child support? Because he feels guilty and wants to do the right thing? Is making me go away the right thing? Phooey! It stinks and it will always stink! Was money involved? Maybe his daddy is footing the bill for Sperm Jr.'s indiscretion. Here they are, all three of them, a very strange trio, tiptoeing out of town on a false pretext. As for me, I'm just tagging along for the ride. As if I have a choice!

The story concocted to explain Mama's phony move to Chicago was that she'd be going to a new job with better pay and greater opportunity. It would be later the non-engagement would get called off due to the difficulties of a long-distance courtship. That's the way it was in those days. Shame, lies, secrecy, and banishment. Cover it up and make it go away. No family member or neighbor can ever know. Gossip like this would be just too delicious to ignore, especially in a quiet mid-western town where a Catholic university's influence ran far and wide.

"If either of you ever speaks of this to anyone, and I do mean anyone," she warned, "there will be hell to pay! It will ruin each of our family names. Do you hear me?" She wagged a finger in his face and then turned to inflict the same upon Mama. "Once that baby is born and given away, life can continue as if nothing ever happened." There was silence as she hesitated to consider her next words. "You, young man, can say one thousand Hail-Mary's or whatever you do to be absolved. ... I don't give a damn. Just don't go forth absolved and do it all over again!"

Giving a baby away wasn't going to make the slate clean, but that's how unwanted pregnancies were solved back in the Fifties. Gramma seemed convinced giving me up for adoption was the right thing, the only thing to do. Of course it's what the sperm donor, the devout Catholic, wanted as well. It got him off the hook. I can't really blame him too much. He was a product of those ignorant times also. Nevertheless, Mama and I were stranded, soon to be separated, left to cope with a decision ostensibly made by others for the rest of our lives. Absolution, adoption? Neither would make the anguish of what was about to happen go away. Who was fooling who?

The snow squeaked and creaked beneath the white-walled tires as it came to a slow stop outside The Cradle Society, Home for Unwed Mothers. Two fresh-faced thirty-something-year-old women trotted down the snow-dusted stairs to greet us curbside. They were twin visions in white with brown fur-lined snow boots pulled over their white stockings. Each wore identical starched white pinafores with white long-sleeved collared blouses and cotton-candy-colored cardigans. And were it not for the little hats perched comically on top of their heads with a gazillion bobby pins, they might have easily been mistaken for ghosts. Toothy smiles of lipsticked lips discharging phony cheer made them ghoulish in the fog. I could feel Mama recoil, so I did too. When Sperm Donor leapt out of the Chevy to shake their hands, he slipped and fell to his hands and knees. As he did so with arms and legs spiraling every which way, a fat envelope fell out of his coat pocket and skated across the sidewalk.

"Excuse me," Mama murmured. "Is there a ladies room I can use?"

"Come, dear. Let's get you inside. The others can follow," one nurse said.

Sperm Donor, having regained his footing, as well as the fat envelope, pressed it into the other nurse's hands and said loud enough for even me to hear, "That ought to take care of everything. Lemme know if you need more." He then turned toward the car and motioned my gramma to follow. "Come. We need to get going. I don't want to get home too long after dark."

Mama stopped on the stairs and turned around when she heard the car doors clunk closed. Marooned on the slick pavement were her three suitcases and canvass knitting bag, the needles poking out like antennae. She watched as the Bel Air pulled into heavy traffic. All too quickly, the car carrying her former sweetheart and estranged mother disappeared from view while gusts of steam billowing through manholes in the street swallowed them up. Mama turned back towards the front entrance and curled her arm under her belly to lift me off her bladder. But it was too late.

"Oh, my!" whispered the nurse standing next to Mama and me. A small yellow puddle was melting the snow between Mama's feet. "Come along, Dearie. Let's get you settled."

With neither a word nor a tear, Mama entered the building, still cradling her belly. Her panties were soaked, her spirits were crushed. And me? I lay very still.

I can only imagine the isolation Mama must have felt when not just the Sperm Donor, but her mother also abandoned her on the doorstep. Mama's new home was such a cold and austere Victorian building. Stone and dark recesses loomed overhead. It was located on a noisy corner in an utterly unfriendly part of the city. Here the landscape was made up of angular surfaces without character or magic. She found herself alone and far from home. Far from the farmhouse where she grew up amidst geese in the front yard and flowering shrubs in colorful disarray crowding around the front steps. Oh how very homesick she must have felt, but she could never go back home now. Not after this. I have no doubt a part of her heart slammed shut that day. I bet she vowed to never allow anyone to ever hurt her ever again. I know I did.

BEFORE LEAVES FALL ON MOUNTAIN LAKE

October is usually about heading south to warmer climes. Canada geese emigrate in formation while honking in chorus. Monarchs flutter all the way down to Mexico, their fragile wings of silky gossamer as strong as a ship's sails. However you, dear Grampa, migrate north to chilly Wisconsin. Every year Mountain Lake beckons your tired soul with promises of rest. It's nothing but a hidden oasis encircled by dense forest in the middle of the vast North Woods, but this is where the heavens reach down to hold you in her gentle embrace. Where you seek renewal and are always restored.

Each morning, in the blue hour that is dawn, a mist will usually rise from the lake, a sheer, flat surface as clear as unbroken glass. Fog swirls in gentle puffs. Constantly in motion, it lifts, falls or suddenly disperses like Indian spirits being chased away by your white-man presence. Save for the drip drip drip of your paddle as it is lifted from the water to reach for the next stroke, your wooden canoe slides across the lake without a sound. The low flat hull seems to slice the water and part the vapor like a knife. You imagine this is how the Chippewa and Menominee fished these waters a century ago and are contented in the emulation of their example. Soon a mesh of stars in a dome of inky indigo becomes extinguished one by one as the sun begins to paint the sky with amber daylight.

You drift with rod and reel parked across the gunwales and a thermos mug of steaming brandied coffee cupped in your hands. All around you, a woodland caught between life and death tumbles down to greet you in wild silence. A vibrant palette of primary colors and evergreen are reflected at the water's edge. Images are doubled – one real, the other a mirrored duplicate in which you actually float. Graceful hemlocks tucked in a cool cove, bow as you slip by. Sylphlike tamaracks compete with quaking aspens. Florescent yellow heart-shaped leaves shimmer against blue-green tufts of short needles in a dance celebrating the new day. But it's the sugar maples with their spectacular leaves of red and orange that catch your breath. I know how much you wish you had a bucket and a tap for collecting that sweetest of nectars. But the hillside is too steep and you are lame.

When you paddle back to the boat house, you pass under a willow whose elongated branches and feathery leaves caress your whiskered cheeks. With a sudden splash an otter dives from its hiding place among moss-covered rock. Half-eaten perch and bass lie rotting, the putrid stench making you cover your mouth and nose. Nevertheless, your suspicion he'd be there today is confirmed, so you laugh heartily. Echoes of your joy ricochet across the lake.

Mountain Lake is definitely your sanctuary. After a semester of bloviating congressmen and a stubborn ideologue for president, I don't blame you for seeking solitary comforts in the wilds of northern Wisconsin. Autumn is the season of hibernation, but for you it is a time of rejuvenation. Your old wicker creel might be empty at the end of most mornings, but not so your soul.

TWO AUNTS IN THE ATTIC

Aunt Annabelle and Aunt Olympia, two peas in two distinctly different pods, lived upstairs in our attic. They moved in when I was seven, when both their husbands suddenly drowned together in the Colorado River. Apart from sharing simultaneous widowhood, their similarity only stretched as far as a maiden name and a childhood plantation home where the ferns grew fat, webs of kudzu clung to both banks of Left Foot Creek, and Cyprus trees dripped with floating veils of Spanish moss.

I always knew which aunt was on the move by her unique footfall over my head. Aunt Annabelle, slim and as lithe as a ballerina, glided across the wooden floorboards with ethereal grace, while her older sister, Aunt Olympia, heavy-set and ungainly, fairly stomped. It was as if she demanded to be heard, while the other preferred to go unnoticed.

Every morning Aunt Annabelle laid out a mat of variegated stripes smelling a bit like patchouli oil and performed thirty minutes of exercise. Her supple limbs, lean and limber, were graceful and swift. She worked in silence and without pause, her breathing but a soft whisper. When finished, she would dab at the beads of perspiration across her wrinkled brow, the loose folds of her neck, and her upper lip which was lined with those peculiar vertical rifts. Then she'd sit on the arm of her shabby sofa, sip fresh pulpy orange juice from a small glass, and stare reverently at Mount Evans' snow-capped peaks.

Aunt Olympia would shuffle and galumph to the bathroom in her dead husband's worn slippers and frayed robe. She would vigorously brush her teeth while humming a tune from Beethoven's *Eroica*, gargle sonorously with minty mouth wash, and slap her cup down on the porcelain sink with the exaggerated gasp of a barroom bruiser. Large hands would rake through her short-cropped grey hair when she glanced in the mirror before returning to the room where she would step over her sister lying on the floor and mutter a profanity. "Dammit, old girl, you need to bloody well get a life!"

Olympia was a concert pianist, stern, humorless, straight-backed, always dressed in men's clothing, and glared over the frames of her eyeglasses. She ate heartily, was a mouth-breather, and read only nonfiction. Lights out for her was at 8:30 sharp.

Annabelle wore polka-dotted dresses and loved to dance, play cards, piece picture puzzles together, and prank her friends. She ate sparingly, pecking at her plate like a bird, read romance and mystery novels, and liked to stay up past midnight.

I loved and respected them both, but it was Aunt Annabelle who always made time to play hide 'n seek with me or go on hikes in search of munchkins living in toadstools or fairies fluttering in and out of Indian paintbrush. Oh, how I miss her so!

GRAMMA'S CABIN

Gabby's cabin looks forlorn, her shutters askew and facade sagging. But in a clearing of wild grasses whose slender blades bow under the weight of an early morning dew, happy memories come flooding back. Everywhere, filaments of spider webs dot the ground in milky white tufts just like the ones we used to snuff when we were kids. They catch the light and shine for just a moment. Our blackberry bushes are still there, too, all in a tangle now. Oh, how we used to scavenge those berries, their purple juices staining our cheeks and clothes.

The cabin has lost her shape. Her posture is bent as if burdened by time. Her complexion, once a burnished umber, is now pale, almost sallow. Too much exposure to the sun has stripped her wavy-edged siding. Under the eaves, the carved corbels, capped in copper, are all rotting. The double hung windows are completely opaque from years of dust and pollen. No longer windows which look out, they are more like the eyes of an old woman whose cloudy vision is compromised by cataracts, her sight turned inward.

I hesitate at the front door, her screen off two of its rusty hinges. Her stained glass transom windows above my head are obscured by abandoned birds' nests. I imagine Gabby swinging on that very same porch bench over there, watching a brood of cousins play in the yard. And when I peek inside I can see the roses twining across the wallpaper, hear a fire in the grate pop and crackle as sparks shoot up the chimney. The air inside is stale and musty now; no scent of lavender or tiger lilies like back then.

Long ago, those first crisp days and nights of fall were always the best. It's when we canned berries, made jam and baked pies. It's when we scampered to the attic filled with dusty surprises, such as discarded clothes for dress-up; photo albums to pour over faces of ancestors we didn't recognize; and a doll house, a perfect replica in miniature of our grandmother's much beloved cabin.

As I turn to leave, wondering if I should bring this place back to life, I glimpse a few deer bedded down at the outer rim of the glade. They watch me with big brown eyes rimmed with long dark lashes.

"Okay, Gramma. You win! I'll stay and fix up this old place."

Carolyn Campbell

PATTY'S MOM

Looking back through the trees flashing summer sun, I see Patty, my bed-bouncing, tree-climbing, fudgsicle best friend. A summer cloudburst has stopped. Under the trees, dripping globes of sun, Patty and I, in our look-alike yellow slickers and red rubber boots, pose for a photograph in front of Patty's house. The phonograph blares Xavier Cougat's rumba rhythms through the open window. *Oh tico tico tic, oh tico tico tic, oh ticoticoticoticotico tic...* Patty's mom is taking the photo.

The sun rains down her Brenda Starr chestnut curls in a river of light. She is wearing pink pedal pushers, a flowered blouse tied in the midriff, and on her feet, Mexican huaraches – huaraches! Her big toe, painted popsicle-red, peeks out at the top like it has a secret.

"Say cheese, say cheese pleeeze, say squeeze me pleeeeze." She laughs through her Juicy-Fruity, movie star lips. "Damn! That's the last picture. I wanted you to take one of me. Oh, well."

Through our window next door, mother, practicing Bach, measures out her life – strong, precise, with no mistakes. Mother doesn't wear huaraches, but sensible shoes and hose even on wash day. She wears a cotton candy-striped, blue-checked, or floral house dress with big sleeves that come three to a package from Montgomery Ward.

Patty and I plan to wade the gutters to Park Hill Drug Store to buy a Black Cow Caramel candy bar, a Bit-o-Honey, or a Jaw Breaker – that small, cement golf ball of sugary yellow, blue, and green swirls, and at the center a chewy chocolate prize.

"Here's a quarter, girls," Patty's mom says. "Buy me a pack of Lucky Strike cigarettes, honey, and a treat for the two of you."

The worms stretching across the sidewalk are more exciting than the gutters' gushing torrents, so we tie our middle legs together with

Patty's mom's perfumed scarf, and with our arms around each other and holding one umbrella, we hobble and lurch our way to the store. We have learned the rhythm of maneuvering three legs. One short step, one long stride. One short step, one long stride. We shriek when we misjudge and end a poor worm's journey.

Under our umbrella, we see the world with eyes open wide to the newness of life, the freshness of each day as though it were washed in rainwater. Arm in arm we explore the neighborhood, the alleys and garage rooftops; we know how to walk the picket fences to the overhanging plum tree in the witch's backyard; we know where the hollyhocks grow wild in the vacant lot and where to dig for broken colored glass for our collection. We know a secret hideout under the low branches of the pine tree where we eat peanut butter sandwiches, decode secret messages from our Dick Tracy rings, play Monopoly, or, if Patty has her way, read Nancy Drew mysteries while I draw or color. We share everything, all of the secrets.

"I have a secret, Patty."

"Tell me! Tell me!"

"Last night, my sister and me laid on our bed and spied on your mom and stepdad. The shade wasn't pulled all the way down. Your mom was wearing your red cowboy hat from last Halloween and pretending your dad was a bucking bronco. He kept laughing and saying, 'Ride 'm babe. Atta girl. Keep a-ridin'.' She whooped and hollered and laughed and laughed. They sure were having fun."

Patty looked thoughtful. "They do that a lot. Once I asked Mom what they were doing carrying on that way. 'The rumba,' she said, and danced off into the kitchen."

I was pretty sure my mother and father never played a game called *the rumba.* Patty's stepdad was a Soldier Boy her mom met at the canteen. My dad carried a briefcase and wore black silk stockings held up by garters even when he hoed the victory garden out back.

One day I ran into the house for lunch to find mother dancing in the living room to the Andrew Sisters singing *Rum and Coca Cola.* She rolled her knees in circle eights and her hips followed. She snapped her fingers above her head and tossed her dark brown hair, now free from the rolled hairpiece.

"Mother! What are you doing?"

"I'm practicing the rumba," she said, smiling and gyrating in a circle.

Oh no! The rumba! I thought. "The rumba, mother? The *rumba?*"

"Yes. Patty's mom is teaching some of the neighbors. We're having a few over tonight to learn the steps."

"Daddy, too?" I gasped.

"Of course. Everybody is doing it. It will be great fun."

"Oh, no, mother, you can't rumba! You don't even have a cowboy hat. Why not just play the piano for everyone? Or sing songs? Or play canasta? Everyone likes canasta. Maybe charades?"

I wanted to tell her she wasn't like Patty's mom; my dad wasn't like the Soldier Boy. Patty's mom cooked breakfast in her baby doll nightie and bare feet, and when she crossed the room the Soldier Boy pulled her down on the chair and tickled her until she couldn't breathe. They had fun at Patty's house. They laughed a lot and played popular songs on the phonograph. Our family fun was playing Chinese checkers. On winter nights, or during an air raid, mother, sis, grandmother, and I worked on a thousand-piece picture puzzle while dad read a book too heavy to lift.

My suggestions fell on deaf ears. After dinner, the neighbors came for their lesson. Patty's mom, dressed in red silk and toeless, platformed high heels, swung her hips from side to side, turning her belly into ripples of fluttering, red butterflies. Her rhinestone eyes and the pin in her pompadour flashed fire. In the candlelight, Patty's mom flamed. She sang *Rum and Coca Cola*, rolled her r's on the r-r-r-um, clicked her tongue singing *tico tico*. The dads clapped their hands and took turns learning the rumba. My dad smiled, showing all his teeth. A battalion of moms in sturdy shoes and well-made wools lined the walls, and when the music turned soft and slow, they watched the butterflies dissolve into fluorescent fish undulating red fins across Patty's mom's buttocks, waver around her liquid hips and swim down her thighs.

Then one hot afternoon, Patty's mom sent her to stay with her grandmother for a couple of days. Making paper doll clothes helped pass the lonely hours without my best friend. In the cool of my room, I listened to the languid sounds of *Sentimental Journey* from Patty's mom's window, playing over and over and over. All afternoon it played, "Gonna take a sentimental journey, gonna set my heart at ease, gonna take a sentimental journey and relive old memories..." Finally, the music stopped.

After dinner, my dad called me out onto the porch. In the silence of the summer night, he held my hand, drew on his pipe and looked up at the stars.

"I have something to tell you. You will have to be very grown up now." The smoke from his pipe curled above his head and disappeared. "Patty's mom is dead. She committed suicide this afternoon...took her own life. Sleeping pills. Patty's stepdad found her when he came home late afternoon. I'm so sorry, honey. So sorry."

My world shattered. All the stars fell out of the sky. My dad put his arms around me and let me sob and shake, unable to comprehend the first tragedy to enter my life. Patty, my forever friend would never be the same. Nothing would ever be the same again.

Dad held me tightly. "They told Patty her mother had an attack of appendicitis and died on the operating table. I wanted you to know the truth, but you will have to keep this secret from Patty until her family decides to tell her themselves. Can you do that?"

"Yes," I sputtered.

Keeping a secret from Patty was a huge burden, a terrible lie that I had to hold while we grew up, a lie that changed my carefree times with her. I kept my promise and never told her the truth of her mother's death. What happened to Patty is a whole other story, not a happy one. She moved away, got polio, and disappeared from my life.

I have thought about Patty and her mom my whole life. The grownup world of love and death, sex and desperation, friendship, loss, and profound loneliness and sadness opened up to me through

Patty and her mom. Memories swirl around me like blowing leaves on a summer day, little deaths that break from the mother tree and fly away. When Patty left my life, she left a hole in the beginning of a lacy world. I had to face a new reality: life is temporal, fleeting, and can come and go like a sudden summer cloudburst. I had to learn over the years the sun does reappear. Yes, it does. It always does.

THE COLOR OF WORLD WAR II

The pale winter sun leaned into the dining room on a cold December morning. Mother sat on the window seat over the radiator drinking her coffee and listening to a soap opera while I picked through a coffee can with stubs of paperless crayons, hoping to find a pink one to beautify Snow White in my coloring book.

Suddenly, Helen Edler, a neighbor and my mom's best pal, burst through the front door, her face tight with fear. "Florence, turn on the news!" Mrs. Edler, usually so fun-loving, always calling my mom *kiddo*, now displayed urgency. "We're at war! The Japanese have invaded Pearl Harbor! War, Florence! Roosevelt has declared war on Japan!"

I wasn't sure what war was, but I knew people fought and killed each other, and names like Hitler and Nazi on the other side of the world were the enemy. Japan and Hirohito, in the shadows for me at that time, now were the enemy too. On that December morning, my mother jumped up, spilling her coffee on my coloring book, leaving a forever brown stain on Snow White.

I suppose the fright in the air that dark day is why I clearly remember my mother and Mrs. Edler, their adult female world, even the flavor of the nineteen forties. Every morning Mrs. Edler joined my mother to drink a cup of coffee, smoke Chesterfield cigarettes, and listen to Stella Dallas, their favorite soap opera. They were pals, all right. They even dressed alike in cotton house dresses with puffed sleeves. There were three dresses to a package from Montgomery Ward – candy striped, checkered, and plain. They both tucked their hair into net snoods. I thought I might like to be like Mrs. Edler, a movie star type on the order of Veronica Lake, lanky and angular, a Swedish blond with dreamy blue eyes and cherry-popsicle lips. She had a throaty cigarette voice and a deep, intimate laugh that held secrets. Her large hands pivoted on her bony wrists as she held her cigarette between long fingers. I practiced smoking my crayons hoping to look like Mrs. Edler.

I remember many images from those days. Everyone living at that time carries stories deeply etched into their lives. Mine are simple, perhaps not worthy of telling, but they are part of the fabric of my life. I was a child who grew up in the shadow of World War II. America mobilized for war. We all became part of the total war and our values, patriotism, hatred of despotism and dictators, and respect for the military are still ingrained in us. Every man, woman, and child worked in some way for the war effort.

We became a red, white, and blue nation, with flags everywhere, *Uncle Sam Wants You* posters, window displays with patriotic Red Cross workers, nurses, soldiers and sailors, WACS, WAVES, and WAFS. Songs blared – *over there...over there...send the word, send the word over there...that the Yanks are coming, the Yanks are coming, the drums rum-tumming everywhere...*

We lived on the corner of 26th and Holly Street. 26th Avenue was the route the caravans of troops, army trucks, tanks, and ambulances headed for the Fort Lowry military base, and further on to Fitzsimmons, the military hospital awaiting wounded soldiers. I stood on the corner waving a small flag when the soldiers passed. They waved back and whistled. My brownie troop sent care packages with cut out cartoons from magazines pasted into scrapbooks. Once I inserted a pressed autumn leaf, a gift from a maple tree which I thought was beautiful.

In school we said the Pledge of Allegiance with our hands over our hearts, our faces somber. At recess, we no longer played Cowboys-and-Indians, but Germans-and-Japs, firing ice ball grenades from behind snow packed fortresses. We raised the flag, marched, and sang...*So prepare, say a prayer, send the word, send the word to beware...We'll be over, we're coming over, and we won't come back 'til it's over, over there.* And so it happened just that way.

Households could only buy meat, sugar, oil, gasoline, flour, lard, tires, and other scarce items with the little green stamps in government-issued ration books. We learned to live with shortages. School children collected newspapers from the neighbors, piling them onto rusty wagons with wobbly wheels, bundling them with twine, and hauling them to the school for the paper drive. We brought tin foil peeled from candy and gum wrappers to stick onto the growing tin foil ball in front of the principal's office, and stamped tin cans flat with our Buster Brown shoes for the tin can drive.

Neighbors used every available space to create victory gardens and provide vegetables for friends and family, so that commercial food would be available for the troops. My dad, a gentleman farmer indeed, plowed a large vacant lot from the alley to the street corner. He loved the idea of being a farmer, bought himself a pair of overalls, a straw hat, and a red handkerchief to tie around his neck; however, he always wore his black silk stockings held in place by garters. He studied horticulture, irrigation techniques, how to enrich the soil, the best ways to plant and seed and eliminate pests. And he was good at it. He babied the corn stalks, the climbing green beans, the zucchini and pumpkin patch, the tomato vines, and all the miraculous roots that plumped under the soil – carrots, onions, potatoes, radishes. Every evening after work Dad removed his business suit, donned his farmer's costume, and with hoe, rake, spade, and hose, he patrolled his garden, his chest puffed with pride.

Across the street, Mr. Brede, "the ornery old goat," cultivated his garden, equally as large and luscious as my dad's. In the evening after work and dinner, Mr. Brede, who also wore a straw hat, red bandana, and overalls, would wander over to our garden to check its progress and criticize my dad's farming skill. "My tomatoes are larger and redder than yours, George. Let me give you some advice. Here's how we did it in the old country." The old country was Norway. Mr. Brede strutted up and down our lovely rows of vegetables, plucking off a bean or pea, pulling up a carrot, shaking his head and muttering about the pitiful progress Dad's garden was making. "It's a skill, my boy. Be patient. I'll give you a few tips to help you." The fact was that our garden was equal to, if not better than, Mr. Brede's. Dad burned under his straw hat. He even thought the old goat lugged his fat tomato worms into our vines after we had gone to bed. Every day there seemed to be a new crop of well-fed knobby green monsters oozing over the red fruit. But justice had its sweet revenge. Smiley Junior High School awarded my dad first place for the best victory garden in the neighborhood. Mr. Brede sulked for the remainder of the war.

I was proud of my father. Too old to join the army, he instead became an air raid warden, trained in first aid and emergency procedures in case we were actually invaded. He wore a helmet and an arm band, carried a flashlight, and looked very important as he checked the neighborhood during blackouts.

Blackouts were exciting. Every household covered its windows with black oilcloth that smelled industrial. Not a single light could shine into the darkness to outline the city for the Japanese bombers. Mother, my sister, and my grandmother Marnie lighted a couple of candles and worked jigsaw puzzles or played Chinese checkers. I discovered I could read the board quicker than the others and always won the games. My sister said I cheated.

I loved sitting in candlelight waiting for the all-clear siren and watching our silhouettes flicker on the walls. How little we all knew of the horrors happening around the world.

Dad invited soldiers for Sunday dinners, a way to make them have a bit of home away from home. He often took our family to Union Station to wave goodbye to the troops heading off to Europe or Japan. The young boys moved in khaki lines, slumped against their heavy packs, eating a jelly donut or catching a few winks before boarding their trains. Pretty girls in pillbox hats and shapely suits tucked at the waist kissed their fellas goodbye. And they cried. I watched them kiss and kiss and cry and cry, a grown-up world of sorrow and courage.

One newsreel image haunts me still: a small toddler, perhaps three or four years old, barefooted, naked from the waist down, in the center of a circle of amused German soldiers. He was screaming with terror as the soldiers fired their guns at his feet making him hop and dance...hop and dance. The ghastly images of Dachau, Auschwitz, and other death camps gradually came into the news shown at the movies; they ate their way into our brains, cowered in dark places, and remain there to this day.

Except for a few signs in the windows honoring a fallen son, brother, father, or lover, life went on in a Norman Rockwell everyday way. Dogs ran free and barked at other dogs or the delivery boys. Newborn kittens mewed behind hollyhocks and wild yellow roses that grew in the alley; Mother made pot roast for Sunday dinner; water sprinklers hissed back and forth spraying summer evenings, perfuming the grass; neighbors chatted, we children played hide-and-seek or kick-the-can; Amos and Andy, and Jack Benny, made us laugh on Sunday night radio. We pulverized a red tablet into lard to make it look like yellow butter, and called it oleo margarine. Mother and Mrs. Edler continued listening to soap operas, drank coffee, and smoked cigarettes when they could get them. My stubby crayons became smaller and smaller, or disappeared altogether, and I had to be content with trees, gingerbread houses, and dwarfs colored purple or orange. All was well. I felt safe. But the horror of the dancing child is with me still, ugly and dark like a coffee stain on a coloring book.

SIMPLY HELEN

I never knew my grandfather, Charlie. He floats around in long-ago shadows without a face or personality. So few vague remarks hook to the framework of my grandmother's life, I can only speculate what it must have been like as a wife and mother married to an alcoholic. "He was a good man when he was sober," grandmother said. She really never talked about him at all, nor did my mother.

Charlie worked for "the bottling works" in Longmont, delivering soda pop and beer to cafes and bars in the area. "Have a drink, Charlie, old boy," was a common practice. By evening, I imagine grandfather rattled to his front gate in a rickety wagon and probably zigzagged to the front door, the ebullient bubbles flat, his self-hatred burning into a red face, his fists knotted and ready to strike.

To me, my grandmother Helen, whom I called Marnie, was an angel, a real angel who kept her wings neatly folded and wrapped in tissue after she came to earth and hid them somewhere in our mysterious linen closet. Her large celestial eyes shone with a divine light, so deep and loving, she drew the world to her for comfort and safety.

I was organizing old family papers and letters for a scrapbook when I came upon a gift card, small and faded with a rosy cherub winding a pink satin ribbon across the top,

For My Husband scrolled among the loops. The card was signed, *Helen*. Simply, *Helen*. Not *Love, Helen*, nor *To Charlie*, nor *Happy Birthday*, nor *From Your Wife*. Simply, *Helen*. It was a cold gift card, yet it was saved.

She must have wrapped a present in pretty paper, tied it with a ribbon, perhaps placed it by his dinner plate long after the evening meal had been served and the children put to bed. As the evening shadows drew into the corners of her kitchen, she dipped the pen into the ink and thought how she would sign the little card. So much she wanted to say at that moment. Her thoughts flew back to

Durango where she met the handsome dark-eyed gentleman. "Oh, how he could waltz!" She must have had a heart swollen with years of tears. But angels don't cry. At that moment, she may have wanted to put on her wings and fly away. But angels don't leave. *Helen* will do, she said to herself, and signed her name – *Helen*. Simply, *Helen*.

Kay Crook

BONJOUR PARIS ADIEU MAURICE

As I sit here planning my trip to Paris in May, I am looking at the map of Paris and the memories come flooding in. I find Rue du Four, the little street that was my first address, a pension filled with students. I think back to those first days, the first days of my school year in Paris.

While most of my classmates packed several large suitcases, I packed one large suitcase and had a trunk with most of my belongings shipped. It was easy getting the trunk to the Detroit airport but no thought was given to how I would get it from the Paris airport to the pension. So, the third day I was in Paris, I took Mary, who had been in Paris all summer and spoke French well, and my friend Judy whom I had just met on the flight over, and we went to the airport to retrieve my trunk.

As we were standing at the desk trying to explain that I was there to see about my trunk, I spotted one of the most beautiful men I had ever seen. He had dark, reddish blond hair and the peaches-and-cream complexion typical of French children. He was dressed in a white shirt under a blue-grey sweater and blue trousers. He had that slouchy way of walking like Richard Gere in *American Gigolo*. I was mesmerized and almost speechless when he walked over and asked if he could help. As he directed someone else to check on my trunk and they were asking Mary all sorts of questions, he began quietly talking to me. Before I knew it, he asked for my phone number and if I would like to go out with him.

As he went into another office, I pulled Mary's and Judy's sleeves. "He just asked me out!" They were speechless.

I really didn't expect to hear from him, but in a couple of days the only phone at the pension rang, and it was for me. I tried to keep the conversation quiet, but quickly all talk around me stopped to eavesdrop. It was Maurice asking me out for the next Saturday and wondering if one of my friends would like to join him and his friend Michel. We would be going to a jazz club. At that time, Oscar Peterson was very popular in Paris; rock and roll hadn't quite arrived.

The nightclub was just like you see in the old foreign films. We walked down a short flight of stairs to a small smoked-filled room. Small tables were squashed together so we threaded our way to an open one. It was a night out of the movies.

Almost every weekend for the next couple of months, Maurice and I did something. One warm autumn Saturday afternoon, we went to a small lake, probably in the Bois de Boulogne, a large park on the outskirts of Paris. Maurice rented a boat, I sat in the bow as he rowed around the lake. We then had a picnic lunch in the park, all very much like a Monet painting. Another Saturday afternoon, we went to the car races. Car races in Europe weren't just cars running around an oval track at 200 miles an hour. European races were like the Grand Prix race in Monaco, though we were at a track and the cars and track were smaller than a Grand Prix. The track was asphalt snaking through a field. There were no bleachers, no fences. You just walked around watching the cars screech around the curves and hoped they didn't run off into the grass in your direction.

I realized I was really absorbed in the French way of life when Maurice invited me to dinner at the apartment of one of his friends. He asked me to invite two of my American classmates. He picked us up in his tiny Citroën Deux Chevaux car. The dinner party was a grand mixture, a total of eight people and three languages. Fortunately, most spoke a little English. The coq au vin, a dish that smelled wonderfully of wine and garlic, welcomed us. Like most European apartments, it was small, so small that the dining area was a long booth and to get to the far end of the table you needed to scoot along or climb across the bench seats. This is where we immediately gathered. It was a French dinner like you might imagine. It started with a light consommé and chunks of wonderful French bread followed by a green salad with oil, vinegar and lots of herbs. During each course there was much talking and laughter. Eating slowly allowed our hosts to join us. Red wine flowed with all the courses. I particularly loved the cheese; a little *bleu*, Camembert, and a soft herb cheese. Crisp apples followed by small candy truffles completed the delicious meal. To help digest all this wonderful food, café and a strong *digestif* were served. We helped with the cleanup, finishing around midnight.

Right after this I moved to the dormitory associated with the Alliance Française, one of the schools I was attending. It was difficult to communicate via phone, because Maurice didn't have a phone and I could only take messages. This led to a cooling of our relationship and I was finding it more and more difficult to adjust to a relationship with a Frenchman. Our cultures were very different. Besides, I had met Stephen.

PLAYBOY PICTURES AND THE ANGLICAN CHURCH OF PARIS

European men seemed to like American girls in the '60s. Judy and I were in a class with an English fellow, Christopher. Typically English, Christopher looked a little like Prince Harry, but with wilder red hair. Christopher asked if we would like to join him and one of his mates, Stephen, for a drink after class. That was how I met Stephen.

We were sitting at a café sipping warm red wine on a cold January afternoon complaining about having nothing to do because going out in Paris was so expensive. Stephen and Chris came up with an idea, one that they had been discussing with the vicar of the Anglican Church of Paris. It was a nightclub in the crypt of the Cathedral.

I loved walking up the tree-lined Champs Elysées from the Place de la Concorde to the Place de l'Étoile with the Arc de Triomphe in the center. Though I had walked it many times, I had never realized how close the Arc de Triomphe was to the Anglican Church of Paris, on a side street just past the George V Hotel. The church was behind Le Drugstore, an interesting place with a lunch counter, aisles of perfume, the French idea of an American drugstore.

This church was a large white stone cathedral, austere, maybe even cold, private, closed, and not seeming to welcome anyone. The cold austere feeling traveled inside the church down to the dark crypt beneath. It was called the crypt, but there were no tombs, just a few small domed rooms with rounded open doorways and small odd-shaped windows between the rooms. The crypt was accessible via a small door on the side of the church. One can imagine the French resistance hiding there during World War II, Charles DeGaulle sending information to the British in preparation for the invasion of Normandy.

What could be a better place to have a club for our friends or anyone else we knew? Steve, Chris, Simon, and Axel were going to do most of the work. We were going to transform the crypt in the

Anglican Church of Paris into the hottest night spot around. The crypt was a room large enough for dancing with a little alcove that would serve as the bar and a small room big enough for a record player and someone to spin the records. Chris's dad, who was in the RAF, provided the black parachute we used to lower the ceiling over the dance floor. But what to do with the walls? We wanted something unique to impress our young customers. What do twenty-something boys have lots of? Why, *Playboy* magazines, of course! So we girls, Judy, Ingrid, and I, cut out the centerfold pictures, Miss December with a Santa hat; Miss January with a glass of champagne; Miss June lying in a field of flowers; and many more. The guys, with loving care, wallpapered the large room with the centerfolds.

The first night we were open you could hear, "Oh wow, those are pictures of naked women! Where did the pictures come from, Stephen?" *Playboy*. Our decorating was a hit! We served only red wine and did no advertising, but word got around. Even our first night was packed. As people left they asked, "Will you be here next week? This is great! What a great time we had tonight."

We were open for several Saturdays as word got out. Kids we didn't know started to come. It was okay for a while, but then one night it sadly came to an end. An American with too much money and no sense stumbled down the stairs demanding a drink. It was obvious he was high. I told Stephen I would take him outside and walk him around to see if I could get him sobered up. The first place he wanted to go was Le Drugstore. His dealer sometimes hung out there. We walked through the crowded aisles of Le Drugstore several times but fortunately, no dealer. I brought him back to our club and he disappeared. Stephen said someone went up to the vicar's office apparently looking for money. Obviously, Stephen and Chris had to tell the vicar and that was the end of our club.

The feeling of the club was friendship, camaraderie among young people from England, Canada, Holland, Germany and the U.S. Those friends opened a world for me. They taught me to enjoy different cultures and led to a love of travel. Unfortunately, except for Judy, I have lost contact with all those people.

ROMAN HOLIDAY

Christmas 1965 was certainly different. My classmates had gone to Switzerland with a fellow we knew from our Paris pension. Since one of my professors in Paris provided me with an introduction to a Roman family, I was in Rome for Christmas. Normally, Christmas meant driving to Detroit on Christmas Eve to have dinner with my dad's family, where everyone brought a dish. Then on Christmas Day, my aunt and my mother would trade cooking. No, no big family meal for me that Christmas in 1965. I stayed at a boarding house in Rome, having travelled over the Christmas holiday through Italy and the south of France by myself. The boarding house was owned by a German couple. In the corner on the black and white linoleum sat a small Tannenbaum. There were no lights in the tree, but painted wooden ornaments of red and white and straw animals were tucked among the branches; a little cheer in an otherwise spare room.

I was alone on that Christmas Day. The French girl I met, who showed me Rome from the back of a Vespa, had to mind the children of the Roman family she worked for. The Roman family, while generously inviting me for dinner just before Christmas, was busy with their family and their Christmas celebration.

So, I decided to visit the Roman Forum. I had just entered the Forum when a very Roman-looking gentleman approached me. Roman-looking because he was tall, a little portly and reminded me of the busts of Julius Caesar, slightly bald with a fringe of soft short light brown curls. "Hello. May I help you?" he asked in very correct English. I didn't answer immediately because I had already had warnings and minor experiences with Italian men so I just looked him up and down. "May I see your guidebook? You know there are many inaccuracies in guidebooks. Why don't you let me guide you through the Forum? See these stains on the stones? They are from coins dropped by citizens fleeing the barbarian invasion of Rome." Parts of the forum were just ruins with partial columns indicating the original grandeur. There were more complete buildings such as the Temple of Saturn; the Atrium Vestae; and the Curia Julia, which was once the Senate. Each stop included a detailed history of the site or building and how it evolved over time. I told him I was very interested in Roman history, as I had taken Latin in high school. He was surprised I had studied Latin because even Romans no longer studied Latin unless they were going into the priesthood.

We walked through the Forum, sat on a stone bench sharing a few details of our lives. He said he was a banker. I was not totally sure what that meant, though he did have the look of one with his dark three-piece suit and trench coat. He had been taking a stroll after attending mass in the morning and having a large Christmas dinner. He had not wanted to spend the afternoon with a noisy family. "May I show you more of Rome tomorrow?" By now I trusted him, but unfortunately was leaving for Pisa and Florence the next day. "May I wish you a safe journey tomorrow?" I gave him the time my train would depart.

When I got to the station the next day, I didn't see him, but I chose a seat next to the window, just in case he did show up. When I saw him and opened the window, we had no time to talk because the train was pulling out of the station.

It is now more than forty years later. My year in Paris is a distant but cherished memory. I can't remember the name of the gentleman in Rome. It wasn't Anthony, but perhaps Federico. If I had had time to meet him that next day, would we have developed a stronger relationship? I guess I'll never know.

Martha de Ulibarri

MEAN OLD RIVER

My father's family often prefaced stories: "When we were on the river." The children's earliest memories revolved around the Red River, a major tributary of the Mississippi that winds diagonally across northern and central Louisiana. My father was born on its banks at his parents' plantation, *Rainbow Bend.* The river divided their lives as it separated the upper part of the state.

One Sunday afternoon, my aunt behind the wheel, my grandmother perched in the back seat like a delicate silver bird, we drove down Texas Avenue and across the Red River bridge. My grandmother, her eyes gleaming with anticipation, said, "Mean old river," as though nodding to a respected adversary and acknowledging a kinship developed over many years. And who better than she would know that this seemingly placid water could unleash the power of a coiling, thrashing snake? On more than one occasion my grandparents yielded to its strength, pulling their home to higher ground.

Going southeast along the highway, furrowed fields lay on one side, the levee on the other. A flock of white birds probed the winter stubble. Mallards and blue-winged teal dove behind the levee. A gray fox crossed the road with a swish of tail.

My aunt pulled over at a white stucco building, a general store and post office in a grove of water oak and sycamore. The sign above the entrance read "Howard" in large black letters. My aunt stepped out of the car. As if expecting our arrival, a woman dressed in her best Sunday coat and hat burst through the door. Her dark chocolate face shining, she threw her arms around my aunt and shouted, "You were my mate!" Tears welled and my aunt exclaimed, "Annie Mae," as she recognized the playmate she had not seen in almost fifty years.

Still embracing, my aunt and Annie Mae leaned through the car window to speak to my grandmother and assure her that Josie, the cook at *Rainbow Bend*, and her husband still lived in the same house across the fields.

Sunlight slanted from beneath gray clouds as we drove up the rutted road to a frame house sagging with age. A tall, rake-thin black man wearing overalls came down from the wide porch to meet us. "How've you been, Napoleon," my grandmother asked as he helped her from the car. "Can't complain, Miss Maggie. The Lord seen fit to keep me here," he smiled down at her. She leaned on his arm, and they turned toward a figure in a rocking chair on the porch.

My father had told me of another visit to this well-beloved couple. "Josie came running barefoot across the fields and hugged Mama." But not this time. Josie was blind. My grandmother sat beside her holding her hand and looking into her clouded eyes. We stood back with Napoleon while their soft voices rose and fell.

My grandmother was a young bride in the 1890s when she and my grandfather brought their furniture and household goods to the plantation landing on a flatboat. Red oak and cottonwoods shaded their house. The wide center hall opened at front and back to capture breezes off the water. I imagined my grandmother and Josie on the veranda gossiping as they shelled purple-hulled peas or in the kitchen stirring cream gravy to pour over roasted quail. Josie would have shared the joy at the birth of my grandparents' first child, a little boy, and the sadness when he died four years later. Three children followed, a girl and two boys, but more sorrow shadowed the cotton and corn fields that spread along the river. My thirty-one-year-old grandfather died of pneumonia. My grandmother sold the plantation and returned with her children to her parents' home in a town away from the river.

That Sunday drive was the last time on the river, and I am the guardian of that memory.

Laurie Hill Gibb

GRANDMOTHER'S LEGACY

From Grandmother Mitchell's small velvet book:
The Records of the family of John Wilson and Rosa Nell Mitchell. Four died when only a few hours old. Vanita Mae died at 6 months, 6 days. Myrtle died at the early age of 8 years, 8 days. Today October 4, 1944, Edgar Ralph, Bruce Lee, Florence Marie and Clarence are living.

Sorrow is hidden between the lines of my grandmother's records, a crushed velvet record of endurance, or not.

What is missing from the record are the names of the four scrawny babies, mouths agape, chirping out unlearned words, clinched fists not able to grasp for air, pin-cushion hearts beating rapidly then stopping forever. No names, no genders recorded. No mention of birthplaces on a squeaky spring bed in some farmhouse somewhere. No mention of dates or times.

What is missing is the footprint of Vanita Mae, dead at 6 months, 6 days of age. Died perhaps when her young brother, Clarence, stood in the dirt-packed yard and hung a rattlesnake over the clothesline. The rattling he failed to hear was that of the buggy rolling off the porch.

What's missing is the name of Myrtle Doris Mitchell in her own second grade penmanship before her death at age 8 years, 8 days. No record of the angel of death that rose from the foot of the bed and swept over her feverish body as her mother watched helplessly.

The sepia page tells only of the birth and death of her husband John Wilson Mitchell. What's missing is his shaky name penned by his hand through fits of racking coughs. No mention is made of the painful farewell to the family's Oklahoma farm as they headed to Colorado Springs for treatment. No record of the weary mother in her forward-facing sunbonnet who was despairing and hopeful, a prayer always on her lips. Nothing about the babe in arms and the two young brothers in baggy wool pants made from their father's worn out pairs. No mention of the little toddler who watched the tears roll down her mother's cheeks. No mention of all that was left behind because there was no room in the wagon, only room for flour, beans, dishes, and kids.

What is not told is the lonely nighttime sobs into her pillow, her heart once again laid open. What are not mentioned in my grandmother's record of the family are a sorrowful journey and a woman who found the strength and courage to face another day, in spite of it all.

PARTING DUST

I only know what my Daddy told me when I was already grown. We'd taken the trip to southeastern Colorado so we could visit the homestead where he had grown up in a sunken sod house. I think the suffering in his family must have been buried deep inside him as dry and hard as Dust Bowl cattle bones. As a child of this family, I, myself, was afraid to bring up too much suffering, so I never asked the questions about that story that I wish I had asked.

I couldn't imagine how parents could leave Charles, their 13-year old son, my Grandpa Hill, in an unknown town on the dry Kansas plains. I can only speculate on how it happened.

I imagine that as a child, Charles slept side by side with his other siblings under the covered wagon while his parents and the babies slept above. One hot night when he was having a hard time falling asleep, and the familiar sounds of coyotes yelping in the distance seemed to sound especially mournful, he heard his Poppa's muffled voice say to Mama, "We'll be leaving Charles behind in the next town." Mama had cried.

Poppa had said, "Don't worry. Charles is smart. He'll be all right." And when she continued to cry, Poppa shushed her, "Don't wake the children, now. Go to sleep. We've got a long road ahead." But none of them had slept that night.

The next afternoon, as they pulled into the nameless town, his Poppa said, "Sorry, Charles, but we just can't continue on to California with so many of us. Food is getting low. Money, too. We're so cramped we can hardly breathe. And, we've got to get to California before winter."

"But Poppa, I'm big enough to help with the cattle."

"Yes, but you're big enough to stay behind and work and take care of yourself, too. You've learned how to do a lot of things to earn your keep. We'll send for you when we get to California."

Charles had stood watching them until all he could see was the dust cloud trailing behind, then only the flat horizon with a big sky above.

He got a job helping out the town's blacksmith for a room in the barn and two meals a day. Every day he went to the post office, but there was never any word from his folks.

Years later, my Grandpa loaded his own family of ten in a covered wagon and headed for Colorado where land was available for homesteading. He worked on the dry land farm as a blacksmith, a well witcher, an itinerant preacher, a dairy farmer, and a cobbler. He beat that dry land into fertility, but in 1935 he watched as the dust bowled over and blew it away. He loaded his wife into a handmade wooden camper and headed up the valley. He scoffed at his sons, Leslie and Vern, as they loaded up their own families and headed into the Rocky Mountains to Guffy, Colorado, as far away from the suffocating dust as they could get.

"Can't live on beauty," Grandpa Hill scoffed as he watched them head out with their families in two covered wagons heading up the paved Highway 50.

"Can't live without it," my mother, the isolated artist, must have thought.

Bev Haney

BLUEBERRIES

We hitch Dolly up to the two-wheeled, faded red cart. Mom takes one side, I take the other and we attach all the rings and chains and leather straps to the proper spots. We fling the metal pails into the back along with our water jars and sandwich bags and climb up onto the worn, peeling wooden bench seat. I take the reins, slapping and clucking like an Old West stagecoach driver, and we are off on our berry picking adventure.

The cart wheels rattle down the road, raising clouds of dust as Dolly trots happily towards the woods. Our exuberant collie Mickey darts back and forth in front of us, barking out encouragement.

We are wearing long sleeved white shirts and long pants so the branches of shrubs and thorns of rose bushes and prickly weeds won't get us, and faded yellow straw hats to shield us from the sun. We are glad we will soon be out of the relentless prairie heat and dust and into the cool shade of the woods.

We find a shady spot where we can tie Dolly to a tree, get our pails out of the back of the cart, and climb down over the big wooden wheels. I attach Dolly's rope to a sturdy maple, leaving lots of slack so she can move about and munch the green grass.

This has been Mom's long-time, yearly ritual and she homes in on the blueberry bushes without hesitation, going directly to the best spot. I trot along beside her, swinging my pail, flushed with the contentment of spending time with her, none of my other six siblings vying for her attention...just the two of us.

For a short while we work side by side, our fingers slowly turning blue as we drop the berries into the pails. They make a metallic clunk on the bottom of the empty pails. I soon find myself swinging from the sturdy branch of a nearby oak tree, my hat tumbling from my head. Mom looks over with a smile and drops another handful into the pail. Then my shoes are off and Mickey and I are hopping over the cold, wet stones in the trickling creek that runs in the ravine just a little farther into the woods. The spindly willows alongside it emit clouds of bloodthirsty mosquitoes as we brush against their lacy green branches and soon Mickey and I give up, racing back to Mom, slapping and swatting as little pinpoints of blood freckle my arms. Mickey rolls frantically in the grass, his legs flailing in the air, a golden whirlwind of fur and dust.

As her pail fills and becomes cumbersome to carry from tree to tree, Mom holds out her apron, now a purple satchel edged in bric-a-brac, fills it with berries then returns to dump it in the pail, a cascading blue waterfall.

After my very empty pail accepts a few more purple offerings, Mom sends me off to get our lunches from the cart. We find a shady spot in the soft grass, share sips of water from the glass canning jar, and turn to our jam sandwiches.

This is the finest dining pleasure I will ever experience, just me and my mom seated in nature's most glorious ambience, savoring every mouthful, sharing love, laughter, and a jar of lukewarm water.

CATTLE CALL

The summer months on our big sprawling farm on the Manitoba prairie were a busy time. My father did not care for idle hands *ever*, so my six brothers and sisters and I were never without tasks to do. One of my least favorite was hoeing the potatoes. We had several acres of potatoes, and per my father's explicit instructions we had to remove every weed from between the rows and around every potato or be sent back to do it all over again and maybe this time without the hoe, but on our knees pulling the errant weeds with our bare hands. In the dry, hot summer sun little clouds of dust rose with every stroke of the hoe and clotted your nose and throat and caked the corners of your eyes.

Other chores for me as the youngest of the seven were feeding the chickens and gathering the eggs, trying to avoid their sharp beaks as they puffed up their white feathers while protecting their nests. There was no end of unpleasant tasks my father could think of to keep us busy and in my mind they were all difficult, dirty and monotonous.

But, there was one assignment that I actually looked forward to. As the hot summer wore on, the lush green pastures of spring were eaten down to brittle, yellow straw and the cattle struggled to forage a meal. However, some green grass still remained in the ditches along the dusty country roads around our section of land.

During this time then, my job was to get on my chestnut pony Dolly, and along with our bouncing collie, Mickey, herd the cattle down the sides of the road to get their fill. My Mom would pack me a peanut butter and jelly sandwich, and always a big chunk of cake slathered with thick frosting, along with a jar of cold water wrapped in newspaper to insulate it from the hot summer sun.

I would put on my red, straw cowboy hat, tie it under my chin, sling my leg over the bare back of Dolly, whistle to Mickey, and we would round up the sixty to seventy head of cattle from the pasture and head them down the road and into the ditches.

It was a wonderful, peaceful time, as I knew I was free for the whole day. My father would be busy in the fields and I would be spared from turning to find him disapprovingly observing my work, veins popping on his forehead while spewing out his favorite invective: "You stupid idiot, can't you do anything right?" No, I would be alone, my whole day ahead of me, on my own!

The cattle were very calm and went about their grazing, slapping their tails to the beat of the flies, exchanging the occasional moo with one another, gradually moving forward down the long expanse of prairie that stretched to the horizon, the rising heat on the road forming mirages of ocean waves in the distance. My only job was to see that they stayed in the ditches and not on the road to allow for the rare occurrence of a car driving by, and to make sure they didn't find a hole in the fence and get into our fields of grain.

Since this was a slow moving procession, I had plenty of time to daydream. I would drop the lines of the bridle onto the ground and Dolly would graze also, I would lie on the soft, green grass and gaze up at the clouds floating by. Mickey the collie would lie by my side occasionally licking my face or hand to make his presence known and elicit a few strokes on his waiting head. Occasionally he would jump up to chase a scolding gopher, then come back to flop down again with a sigh.

Gazing up at the wispy clouds, the hot sun raising little trickles of sweat between my shoulder blades and under the rim of my hat, in my reverie I took trains to far-away places, conductors nodding to me between puffs of steam, as I climbed up the steps in my yellow hat with the pink rose, my gloved hands clutching my matching purse. "All aboard!"

I took a bow as adoring fans leapt to their feet at the conclusion of yet another successful piano concert. I sipped wine with my handsome suitor with the pencil thin moustache and the gold cigarette holder at the round glass table in my apartment in the big city of Winnipeg. A wealthy businesswoman, enjoying a rich social life.

A quick bark from Mickey or a sudden jump by one of the cows, causing a bovine chain reaction, would jolt me out of my reverie.

Sometimes now, when I hike up the rocks to my craggy mountain sanctuary, I will sit down on a rock, look up at the drifting clouds and my nostrils suddenly fill with the sweet, sweaty smell of my precious pony and I feel Mickey's loving wet tongue on my hand.

Once again, I am ten years old and I am a cowgirl.

STORM SHELTER

Outside on the cold Canadian prairie a storm was brewing. As the snow fell, the wind picked it up and blew it in white sheets past the frosty windows of our farmhouse. It continued until it met up with a barn or a shed where it would pile higher and higher, swirling into frigid sparkling sculptures. There was no indication that there were roads out there except for the dim outline of fence posts hunched against the wind. No one was going anywhere.

In the parlor my mother sat down at the old upright piano, the top a clutter of family pictures haphazardly placed on Grandma's doilies. One by one we were drawn to the sounds, putting down our books or games without prompting, and soon we were all gathered around, shirttails hanging, bony knees poking out of ragged jeans, a rag-tag farmer's choir.

This was a special time when we didn't try to stay out of Dad's way for fear of a reprimand or an order to get to work. We were all one musical unit. We would glance out of the corner of our eye in Dad's direction and perhaps see a smile of pride as our voices filled the parlor. This was a special time indeed!

Dad would sing bass as he so proudly did in the church choir. My three sisters sang harmony accompanied by much giggling as they figured out who sang which part. I don't think they knew the names for the parts, they just sang what sounded right. The two oldest, Irene and Ruth, sometimes sang together at a church or school function (Dad beaming in the audience) so they had an idea of what worked. Lois, the younger sister, exhibiting her natural ability, easily joined in. Howie, the middle brother, sang beautiful tenor harmony, too and Len, the youngest brother, liked to think he was an opera singer and sang with great gusto and expression. Wally, the oldest, was more serious and shy and didn't sing out, but probably was humming quietly in the background.

As the youngest, I loved to join in and was quick to burst into fits of giggles at the slightest provocation. It was a glorious time and I loved to be part of this special family, happy voices in harmony all around me, laughing, touching, loving each other through music. We all knew tomorrow it was back to work. Everyone had their jobs to do and it was serious. No fooling around. But for now our voices filled the cozy parlor as we drew together and drowned out the howling wind.

Patty Hollow

EMPTY HOUSES

The sunlight, gloriously bright, bounced across the rainbow strip of beach. The waves rolled in soft, fat curves, a set of seven perfectly formed, while the surfers waited for their turn with urgent expectation. The fragrance of the salty wetness reminded me of something from my childhood, strange but oddly pleasant. A moment to remember, a burst caught in the neurons as it sifted like the papery sand through my fingers. Was I two years old again before real memory begins, or was it just a cellular imprint from old photos and dry whispers by my crib? I didn't know.

She wore a blue and white checkered kerchief tied under her chin, wrapped around curly blond fly-away curls. She smiled and handed me the empty home of a hermit crab. The brown and white striated shell was rough and bumpy on my soft, new hands. We sniffed the fishy cave together and made *funny faces* to each other; a sweet child-like moment. She handed me a twig of driftwood so I could poke it around in this empty shell.

We walked further along the shore, and when the rocks got too big for me to walk on she picked me up, piggy-back style and I giggled with delight. I blew tiny breaths into the hollow core when she showed me how to play this game, and the shell became a soft whistle with random notes of sea sounds.

The sun was softening, the tiny bubbles of foam tickled, breaking over our toes, big and little footprints that were washed quickly away in the soft lapping waves. Still it was a long day of sensory delights, a full spectrum of memories for two lives that crossed only a few times and only once on that bright beach day when the light was so iridescent and so glorious.

The end was just weeks away before she left, leaving behind the skeleton crab house that was no longer filled, abandoned to make room for a new owner.

FIRST WORDS

"Has lots of rhythm will probably be a good dancer." The tiny script, recently found in an old baby book, jumped out at me. I could barely read it, the scratchy print diluted with age and mold, a little footnote that caused me to hold my breath for a moment and reread what I thought I saw. My eyes filled with tears. Not really a significant statement, just a short sentence, and it sent me reeling. I remember pouring over her few old photos, a dreamy, whimsical girl who looked like a Renaissance angel with long, wavy blond hair and an enigmatic smile which didn't reach her eyes. She appeared to be looking at something far away.

She left me right after I took my first steps and probably the only photo of us together was of a baby clinging to her skirt in that slightly unbalanced, drunken way that toddlers often do. I appeared to be in a sour disposition as I scowled into the camera, my elf ears peeking out of flattened mousy brown hair; it's no wonder she left. I was such a contrast to her ethereal, golden beauty that it seemed unlikely to me on appearance that I was hers. I didn't look much like my father either. Maybe, I'd been switched at the hospital; it was not completely uncommon in those first baby booming days when women were popping babies out like flies in understaffed postwar hospitals. This was a childhood fantasy: that my real parents would appear and I would start a real life.

My child's mind was half convinced that I didn't belong there, particularly since she was talked about in whispers. She became invisible and so did I. The truth was harder to understand, she actually left me for another man and that was a really bad thing or so everyone said. My father's mother said I should be grateful that I had someone to care for me since my mother had all the morals of an alley cat, which made her particularly loathsome since Grandmother hated cats.

My poor unknown mother didn't have much of a second life with her new husband. She died in childbirth right away, and since everyone felt she got what she deserved, the subject was never mentioned again, and I never could ask.

I just recently heard a wonderful haiku from an ancient Japanese proverb which said, *A silent death is an endless worry*. It stopped me in my tracks; all the unknowns in a *forever sort of way*. So her first words to me were her last words, but long ago she knew something, a little thought she wrote down and it became a part of me. I do have rhythm, and I could dance the night away.

WATER GIRL

I got out of that house lickety-split every day of that summer. I grabbed the change that poor, dotty Nana had left me on most mornings; an inconsistent spate of nickels, dimes and pennies left on the nightstand. By that time, she was already on the pier playing Bingo with an odd assortment of mumbling characters whom she attracted and paid for. We were like ships passing in the daylight, each on her own mission. Once in a while she would go to the grocery store to make one of her *famous pies* but then she would forget and leave out the ingredients until they spoiled; and I think once she did actually give us a bout of food poisoning, but at that point I did not care. I had discovered hot dogs, cotton candy and snow cones. A true bounty to a child who was raised on tea, roast mutton, and Brussels sprouts.

Just before summer, my real mother had died and I was sent to spend time with her grieving mother, my never-before-seen-Nana. *They*, the other part of my family, thought it was a swell solution to a bereft mother and a misplaced child. *They* didn't know it made no difference to Nana or me. My mother left us all years before on a romantic escapade and never looked back. I only saw her once about a year before she died, and it was a vague memory of a plunge on a navy base, holding a baby in her arms. I think she taught me how to swim that day because from that moment on whenever I was near water my heart burst with a desire I didn't understand and the lure was like a sailor at sea spotting his first mermaid. I just jumped in head first!

TREASURE HUNT

On that special California day that was almost gone, I explored every bit of my beach. There was one hobo in particular who loved to get into the trash bins chained to the boardwalk. He would dig with such ferocity that when he found something great he would spit on a dirty rag and clean up a smashed Kewpie doll or chipped ceramic cat with such tenderness.

"Oh Yeah!" he chuckled, furtively hiding the toys in his burlap bag.

After the ocean and after dusk I went to the pier, a cacophony of sounds and colors, balloons and rhinestone-studded globes twirling on the clapboards to entice the customer. I loved watching the veiled ladies with big breasts and fat red lips and tiny dancing dogs in turquoise jeweled collars and clown hats with their ears popped out. I loved it all!

If I had an extra nickel I would go over to the glass cage with iron jaws that could pull out a true treasure if it were grasped just right. Sometimes it was a plastic doll with slanted eyes, but the best was a filigree ring with a gigantic ruby on it, a *wishing ring* to tell my future.

When I was late, the guy on the corner would give me a cold hotdog on a soggy bun. "Hey Cutie, this is for you," he would wink and hand it to me as he closed shop for the night. Even cold, the hot dog popped in my mouth, spitting salty, oily water out of its tight pink skin. What a sensory delight! What a perfect moment! Fingering the *wishing ring* in my pocket, I skipped through the alleys and canals of Venice Beach winding my way backwards to my temporary home.

Marcia Jones

NAMELESS

In the sticky summer of 1968 a top-ten hit beat its rhythm and swirled its lyrics through my head while I worked on an assembly line to pay for college.

All the world over, so easy to see.... People everywhere just want to be free.... I can't understand it, so simple to me.... People everywhere just got to be free.

That summer I met a mysterious woman whom, due to my innocence and youthful lack of empathy, I did not understand. She haunts me still.

Veiled in her dark memories, she stood beside me that steamy, overcast July. We installed parts into record changers all day long in the factory's raucous, mechanical din.

Tall and fragile, her long dark hair was dull and strung with filaments of white. Her sleeveless dresses were old, faded, and neatly pressed until the daily humidity took its toll.

Her thin arm bore a tattooed concentration camp number, and it stared at me with defiance. I felt its vile horror chill me like slow dripping icicles in November. I had never known anyone who was in a death camp.

Finally she, hoarding unspeakable secrets, splintered our silence and reached out to me, a selfish, naïve, young girl. We talked about our jobs, the weather, my school, and my boyfriend. She told me she was from Lithuania, a place I knew nothing about.

We were both shy, and I did not ask questions. She carried loss on her narrow shoulders, and I was afraid to probe.

Now I wonder how violence and fear did not break you. What memories, dreams, and hopes did you leave behind? Did you lose a lover or a child? Did any of your family live? Did friends or neighbors collaborate to betray you? Did you escape, or were you liberated? How did you end up on the shores of Lake Michigan?

Where was your line between hatred and acceptance?

I know now that 94% of Lithuanian Jews were murdered in the Holocaust.

You survived.

I can never forget your dusky Baltic eyes like sunken lakes of bruised violet. Yet, after almost a half century, I don't even remember your name.

WHAT HER HEART DID NOT HOLD

The day after death set my mother free, I unlocked the drawer of her nightstand. In it I found keys to her mysteries, but what I did not find would change my outlook forever.

I found old letters, yellowed, and tied in plump bundles with faded red ribbon. I found brittle child custody papers arrested in a tatty rubber band. And I found her gold music box that still played *Que Sera Sera, Whatever Will Be Will Be.*

Lying in silence underneath the papers I found her old handmade wooden box with tiny brass hinges and a crooked inlaid M. I imagined my father crafting this delicate box more than one-half century ago to hold my young mother's dreams.

I imagined him peeking around the trunk of an oak tree holding the box hidden behind his back. She flirted and tried to take it from him. He, tall, innocent, and oh so handsome, and she, dark eyed, oh so pretty and only sixteen, full of anticipation, before their love stars crossed.

I remembered that box resting on her dressing table surrounded by her perfumes and talcum. Her black and white snapshots of new love, her matching comb, brush, and mirror, and her hair clips to pin her extravagant dark hair high on her head.

I opened the heart box. Inside were her thin gold wedding band and a worn old snapshot that captured love's first glow – kept after all the disappointment and crushing passion and sorrow that hit them like the shock of an iridescent bird smashing into a window.

She saved the heart box for herself and for me. Chapters from her story, some still with no end, drifted from that box like thistledown on a windless day.

Stories of her fragile marriage to my father, of her bitter divorce, of her single mom's struggle to work an assembly line all day, of her brave midlife beginnings, and of her hope for a career after her girls were grown.

Stories of whimsy and humor and wit when teaching me to drive or cook, of peace that comes with always being kind and soft spoken, of yearning to make up for self-perceived failures in love, of singing even though she could not carry a tune.

Stories of her fear of the judgment and biting gossip of neighbors and church women. Stories of laughter, of acceptance of endings, and of more friendships than anyone could imagine.

Some stories I did not find. There were no stories of regrets. "*I am dying with no regrets,*" she told me on the last day before her story ended.

THREADBARE MYSTERIES

When autumn makes its sharp turn into winter, and cold nights begin in the afternoons, I always think about Grandma's freezing attic bedroom in the old northern Wisconsin farmhouse where we slept under piles of heavy quilts and blankets. The feeling of security when sinking into a soft bed under the comforting weight of quilts, all handmade by Grandma, is seared in my memory.

I marched up the wine-red winding staircase to the attic where Daddy and Auntie's tiny childhood bedrooms nuzzled under the eaves. It was where I slept when I visited Grandpa and Grandma. I climbed the uneven, wheezing stairs while shivers raced clear down to my feet.

The attic's special scent comforted me with its blend of musty old clothes and books along with nineteenth-century wood that exuded just a hint of Grandma's secret lemon-scented cleaning solution. The gasping fragrance of the cold air trapped in that room completed my welcome.

Under the covers, the cold sheets stunned my body in spite of the flannel nightgown that draped clear to my ankles. Sometimes Grandma surprised me with a hot water bottle to toast my toes.

Crickets inhabited the bed! Dark, shiny, and jumpy as black lightning they chirped at the invasion of a cold child. Afraid of them, I sometimes could not sleep. What if one romped through my hair or slept under my nightgown?

Grandma piled her quilts piled high against the chill. I thought of the princess and the pea, but my quilts were on top of me, not underneath me.

My favorite quilt was threadbare and worn, soft as a fleeting dream. It was a farm wife's quilt, plain and functional with faded squares patched together. In that quilt, my father said could see every cotton handmade housedress my grandmother wore during his childhood. The muted colors of America's depression – sage green, mauve, ivory, and cornflower blue with floral and striped patterns had faded with endless abuse on Grandma's washboard.

The quilt held stories of sorrow and disappointment and tragedy, of comfort and love and home. I imagined these patches reflecting beginnings and endings of truths that unraveled farther than I could see.

Grandma, you wear a staid navy with a tear-stricken bodice the morning you bury your stillborn daughter.

You wear the olive green with deep pink tiny roses when your labor pains start for your first beloved son, my father.

For your first jaunty trip in Grandpa's new black Model A, you sweep out in the newest fashioned wheat and white polka dotted dress, a riding hat added at the very last minute.

You put on a blue, white, and pink paisley dress the day you adopt your toddler daughter, who is homeless after tragedy strikes her family.

You sport a dress with hot pink, blue, white, and yellow flowers splashing on a black background before you invite the preacher and his fancy wife for dinner at the farm.

And you slip on a tan and white geometric print dress as soon as you feel better after the birth of your second son, my uncle.

What are you wearing on the bleak night you find out for sure that my grandpa is having an affair with the silly woman three farms over? It is the white, lavender, and periwinkle print, your favorite, thus ensuring your confidence to confront him at last.

You are on the cusp of the movement for the 19th amendment finally allowing women to vote. For the momentous event, you show off your dress with the ivory background wildly spread with magenta and brown modern geometric patterns. You make your own first voting decision and don't tell Grandpa.

During long depression winter nights, you curl up in your pink and blue plaid to share your profound love of words with your three enchanted children whose feet rest on the kitchen woodstove while, wide-eyed, they soar from that farm to see the world through books.

Haying season means enormous noontime dinners for a dozen ravenous and sweaty men. You wear an old blue and white striped dress and yellow apron to pick onions, corn, green beans, potatoes, tomatoes, and plums. You pluck four chickens. You bake your county-famous cinnamon rolls, mash potatoes, slice mounds of tomatoes, and roll out crusts for plum, lemon, and cherry pies – all produced to perfection with only your wood-burning stove and oven. You fill pitchers with today's cold milk. Just before the noon dinner bell, you change to your dress with red, white, and blue flowers dancing with tan rectangles on a white background.

As you anticipate your 59th birthday, you find out from the doctor clear over in Minneapolis that your unbearable and silent pain is inoperable cancer, and you will only live a few pain-racked weeks. You wear a purple and black dress as armor against the shock.

In a few short weeks you do not wear dresses any more, for you stay in bed, inside your pain, and under your plain quilt with all the memories that may end with you or may never end.

On that torn and threadbare November night in 1959, your story unravels and you let go of your oh-so-young and generous life.

Shock and pain shattered my father and me like a violent fist smashed through a delicate frost-etched window that can never be put right again. I watched my father cry. It was the first time I had ever seen him lost. I chilled with fear that he might be as vulnerable as I was.

I crept up the winding stairs on the night of her funeral, a 12-year old girl carrying doubts and grief and loss up to the cold attic where I buried my head under her quilt and stared for the first time into the dark mystery of death.

Carl Jurgens

LIFE'S DYNAMITE PITS

From my father I learned fear and vigilance. From my mother I learned caution. "Do you really know how to do that?" she would ask me when I happened to mention I was embarking on some new venture or another. In the Marine Corps I perfected my vigilant nature, always being aware of my situation, sniffing the air like some sloe-eyed, muzzle-dripping bloodhound. Anticipating every possible problem that could arise, whether a threat to my family, my person, or my wallet, was the defensive bulwark I maintained. I was convinced that life and limb would be much safer if I pursued such a course. It was exhausting!

I had successfully completed Marine Corps basic training at Parris Island, South Carolina, a subject in itself for another time, and had entered infantry training at Camp Geiger, Camp Lejeune North Carolina. The Marine Corps has always prided itself in selecting the most inhospitable, godforsaken locations on earth to build and maintain its training facilities. I suppose the places where the Corps has found itself in conflict with our country's enemies necessitated such hellholes. Camp Geiger was no exception.

"All right you meatheads, today we are going to have some fun." The range sergeant had a wry smile on his face. "This is a live fire exercise and I don't feel like sending no one home to their mamas in a body bag so keep your friggin' heads down." It was the infiltration course, and we would be crawling from one end toward a machine gun nest. That didn't seem too difficult. The only catch was that interspersed throughout the course were pits, surrounded by a low barbed wire fence, which contained half-pound charges of dynamite. Periodically, these would be set off to simulate incoming artillery or mortar fire. I soon discovered that there was little chance of getting blown up, as it was practically impossible to crawl into one. However, I did notice that every time one was set off it sent out a spray of mud and water saturating anyone close. Therefore, I made it my business to stay as far away as possible. Spotting one ahead of me, I studiously crawled to the side, the whole time keeping my eye on the avoided pit. There was a huge explosion about two feet from me. My body rose up several inches from the ground. I did not suffer any injury from the explosion, but I was covered by a tremendous spray of mud and water.

The experience taught me one big lesson. Oftentimes in this life when you are focusing your attention on one of life's mud holes and you try to avoid it, you find yourself enveloped by another one that you never saw coming or expected.

THE MOUSE THAT ROARED

Was it a proclamation of things to come? Was Olympus speaking out? It was a beautiful summer afternoon. Flowers, long since having blossomed, were still emitting their fragrance from colorful petals encouraged by the warm days and nights of a Colorado summer. In the trees surrounding the primordial B & B where we had gathered, birds chirped their melodious song of summer, happy just to be; free, without care. Pat and I stood before family and friends gathered to give support and love to the union that we were now avowing in words scripted by the Reverend Kathy, minister at Mile Hi Church where Pat and I had met. The fragrances and sounds that emanated from the sylvan surroundings lent an air of pagan ritual to the marriage that we were now proclaiming. Just how pagan we were soon to find out. Sometime during the "I Do's" a screech was heard behind Kathy. She turned, as she was facing Pat and me, and our gathered entourage, to see what had emitted that terrible sound. As a hushed murmur arose a rather large domestic cat proceeded rather hurriedly across the yard about twenty feet in back of Kathy. Suspended from the cat's mouth was an extremely frightened, grey field mouse, very much alive and proclaiming its protestations at being the cat's lunch. The reaction of everyone was mixed. Kathy, being ever the professional, uttered a short prayer for the mouse's repose, and continued to assist Pat and me in completing our vows of eternal fidelity and love.

Fortunately we do not give particular credence to events which could otherwise be construed as harbingers of coming attractions. However, if one were to so do, one might ask whether the rather tragic scene, at least from the mouse's point of view, played out during our nuptials might foretell the drama that one could expect to experience in the coming wedded years. Although there has been the odd scream from time to time, for the most part this event has not been reenacted. When the winter winds begin to blow around our vintage cabin and the field mice begin to seek out the warmth of our porous cellar, I am once again reminded of the memorable day and the event that punctuated our ceremony.

Pat Jurgens

HATING SUNDAY

Who is the little cherub smiling in the photo? You guessed it. Me, in faded pajamas, surrounded by a scattering of clothes and shoes across the scratched wood floor. A bedraggled teddy bear, with fur worn off, lies on the old blond dresser. My bedroom's as Spartan as an orphanage. This is the church parsonage, my home sweet home.

As the smile seems to suggest, I grew up oblivious to bleak surroundings, hand-me-down clothing, or material possessions. I was taught *things* were not godly. After all, my father was a Methodist minister. He didn't have to say a word to me personally. I heard his message loud and passionate from the pulpit every Sunday. We sat in the center of the third row, down front where everyone could see *the minister's family*. I had to be good; I was a small fish in a glass bowl.

No one knew about the screaming fuss I made every Sunday morning in the frenzy before church. I succumbed to the painful pull of hair rags and brushings that preceded the march across the parish lawn. I imagine I was dressed in my little tweed coat with the double breasted buttons and matching bonnet. We slipped into our pews just before the organ exploded in chords that shook the rafters and the choir in their terracotta robes began the processional down the long aisle of the sanctuary.

My voice croaked as I joined in singing *Onward Christian Soldiers*. I squirmed in the hard wooden pew and swung my legs, kicking the seat in front of us. The mayor's wife may have turned and scowled at me.

Perhaps my older sister jabbed me in the side with her elbow. "Shh!"

Mother usually produced a scrap of paper and pencil. "Here, Patty, take this."

I made angry scribbles on it, a stick-figure man on a box with a long pointing finger. Looking up, I saw my father in his long black robe and with a voice that echoed into the corners of the gothic sanctuary. Waving his arms, he looked like God himself, or a large bird of prey. Either way he was a little scary.

"And Jesus said, *do unto others as you would have them do unto you,*" boomed into my ears. I may have confused my human father with the big Kahuna in heaven.

I just know that being a PK (preacher's kid) didn't protect me from Sheila, who beat my head against the ice wall of the igloo in our backyard until I saw stars. I failed to *turn the other cheek,* but I never spoke to her again. And I remember how Susan giggled and pulled down my panties on our way to school. I punched her so hard in the stomach she doubled over in the grass crying. I felt no remorse whatsoever for either retaliation.

These episodes marked the onset of my journey as a closet heretic.

THE GUNJ

The Gunj – a strange and unlikely name for a burst of personal freedom and an afternoon of culinary delight. Nineteen years old, I had traveled halfway around the world to study at a girls' college in India, only to find my freedom curtailed by strict institutional and cultural rules. The Gunj was a local shopping center in Lucknow where female students were allowed to frequent without chaperones.

Permission granted for an expedition, a friend and I whirred along Faizabad Road on a bicycle rickshaw, bell ringing. Awash in a mosaic of sounds, sights and smells, we wove through chickens, a bullock standing in the middle of the road, carts and wagons of every description. Old men wrapped in blankets sat talking under a banyan tree. A monkey-nut seller smoked a hookah pipe on the bridge of the Gompti River. *Wallahs* squatted next to their wares of *puris*, *chapattis* and *samosas*, displayed in glass boxes in a useless attempt to keep away flies. Dung clung to the large wooden wheels of a *bail gharry* drawn by an emaciated ox. A dozen women, children, and old men clung to the moving cart. A *pundit* in a Nehru shirt walked behind carrying an umbrella.

I saw all this and more on the way to the Gunj. The images changed like a kaleidoscope from one moment to the next, a rainbow of bright saris and head turbans. The smell of dung, urine, and curried spices combined with the heat of the sun to besiege my olfactory senses.

Climbing out of the rickshaw at our destination, I paid the skinny rickshaw driver fifty *paisa* for the ride. "Salaam, Baba," he intoned with a smile through missing teeth.

A swarm of small children immediately surrounded us.

"*Ek paisa, Baba?*" they pleaded, holding out dirty hands for alms. Dressed in rags and barefoot, they followed us to the shopping stalls, desperate for some coins from the white *Missahibs*. I once gave a little girl a *paisa* only to be followed for an hour by a covey of children; it was not possible to help them all.

"*Namaste, Missahib*," the shopkeepers greeted us. "Beautiful *chappals*, very good leather. Nice, for you." English was the second language of India, and the merchants knew the words of their trade.

Bargaining was the way of life in the small shops and stalls, and that was an adventure in itself. Today, I was bound for the tailor who would sew me a *salwar kameez*, a comfortable two-piece garment worn by young Muslim girls. I chose a colorful print and was measured with a threadbare tape. The tailor had one sewing machine in an open stall where he sat, rhythmically rotating the foot treadle.

But the highlight of the afternoon was an indulgence at Kwalities, where once through the smoky glass door another world awaited. Inside the marble-floored restaurant cooled by undulating ceiling fans, upper class Indians took tea and pastries or sipped *lhassi*, a lemon yogurt drink. For a foreigner it was the only safe place to have an ice cream. And when the confection appeared in a tall parfait glass topped with whipped cream and a cherry, I was sure I had died and gone to heaven. The cold sweetness melted in my mouth and soothed my lonesome heart from the powerful strangeness of India. The smile it brought to my lips lasted all the way back up Faizabad Road to the college gate.

WIGS: $10 WITH FILL-UP

In the 1960s when I was a twenty-something, we "girls" wore our hair in bouffant hairstyles, or tried to. The beehive, that big soufflé of hair, was the ideal and for someone with fine, thin hair like mine, an impossible attainment. I tried endless methods to make more of my mousy brown locks. I blow-dried with my head upside down and was left with the scent of singed hair and strands sticking in all directions. I teased the ends until the hairs on my head resembled a rat's nest. And I used so much perfumed hairspray to solidify *the look* that inhaling the fumes made me high. But the worst part was sleeping every night on hard plastic curlers pressed painfully against the scalp.

As a young married woman with small children, my days were spent washing baby diapers and chasing after toddlers, to say nothing of keeping a spotless house and welcoming the husband home every night with a bright smile and dinner on the table. The *little woman* with red, chapped hands was expected to manage the household and present herself like a fashion plate at a moment's notice.

One night my husband, who was in the investment business, called after work.

"Honey, having drinks with Guy ... my broker buddy... invites us ... dinner tonight... the Wellshire Club."

"Tonight?" I said, as the dog ran under the telephone cord, and a toddler pounded after it screaming. "Just a minute... Stop it! Your father's on the phone; I can't hear!"

"Get a sitter ... meet me at the Grant Street Pub ... 7 p.m. .... We'll have another ... Hey, Man, how's it going? Honey? Gotta go. See ya at seven."

Frantically, I tried to tease my errant mop into submission. The results were, shall we say... unimpressive.

After one of these episodes, I noticed a sign in the window of the Sinclair gas station. Beneath a green Dino the Dinosaur it read,

"Wigs – $10 with Fill-Up." The station attendant held up a brassy blond wig. I hesitated.

"Do ya want it? It's the last one."

"Yes," I said without trying it on. I was in awe of the volume of cascading curls tumbling into my hands.

Back home in front of a mirror, I pulled the rigid backing down over my head and grimaced. The wig pulled and pinched, settling over me like a vise. I squinted into the glass; Goldilocks stared back at me. This crop of hair needed a shampoo/set at the corner beauty shop. That accomplished, I was the proud owner of a beehive, stiff to the touch but every sticky hair in place.

My first appearance as a blond bombshell came soon enough. We went for drinks and dinner at the Golden Ox, a high-priced steak house in Denver. When I appeared, my husband didn't recognize me.

"Don, it's me, your wife, you're flirting with."

"Why, honey, you're a knockout!" he guffawed in surprise.

I wasn't quite sure whether to be pleased or not, but I felt slightly risqué. It was like being an actress in my own play. Sipping on a Manhattan, I wore a pink miniskirt with a long beaded necklace and dangly earrings below the overwhelming presence of the beehive wig. Dinner had come and gone and drinks were still flowing. The band was warming up with *The Twist*.

"Let's dance." My husband caught my hand and guided me to the dance floor. He was an excellent dancer, quick on his feet, and in sync with the rhythm. We twisted and twirled until I was breathless.

It was a warm summer evening with a single ceiling fan wafting the aroma of cigarette smoke through the room; the air was close. My scalp began to perspire and my head itched. I poked a furtive finger into the fuzz on my head. The cap that held the hair was impenetrable; there was no relief.

The music grew faster, and soon we were doing the jitterbug. As we bopped up and down and swung around, my wig started to inch up. I reached for the tab behind my ears and pulled it back down. It inched up again. I could feel my face and neck getting red. It became a continuous tug of war: me against the wig – up, down, I tried to time it with the music. Twirling under Don's arm, I felt the wig creep across my forehead at a rakish angle. I was terrified that it would pop off and skate across the floor. I'd be left standing with my matted mouse hair for all to see.

Thankfully that never happened. My blond days were relatively short in number, and I moved on to the greater personal freedom of the 70s, with long, curly hair that was my own – yes, it was mouse brown. The drama of being blond with a huge head of hair had been a temporary comic relief. The long-lasting lesson turned out to be learning self-acceptance.

Susan Kerr

THE MEETING

I had been standing by the road for a long time. I knew I wanted to be here, but how and why I could not remember.

Shadows were growing longer, but the day was still warm, quite warm. I took the bonnet off my head. It felt wonderful to be freed from it, and I shook my head. *No. No, this won't do. My short hair will surely betray me.* I put the bonnet back on.

This is the right road, I feel certain. It was more two dusty ruts than a full-fledged road. *Was I really doing this? What would I say to him?* I always imagined that the words would just come. I could never tell him the truth. He wouldn't believe it anyway; nor should he.

I shifted from one foot to the other. The boots were soft and worn, and I was glad for their comfort. I patted the cotton skirt, aware of the many layers beneath it. *How did they possibly work in something so unnatural?*

I saw the two figures as they rounded the bend beyond the far field. I was certain it was him, and Mr. B., his friend, as he always referred to him. *Oh my goodness, they are coming just as I imagined they would.* I picked up my basket and stepped into the road.

They were so young. I read it even from this distance. They were aware of me also, I could tell. Their posture and pace betrayed their fatigue. They were not in uniform. Perhaps the grey trousers were Confederate issue, but their shirts were loose-fitting cotton, and each had slung a rifle over the shoulder with a strap. The man on the right carried an empty sack in his hand. The trim beard told me that it was him. My great-grandfather was walking down this road toward me!

The heat of the day had taken its toll on me as well. My heart was pounding, but an unearthly calm hung in the air on that late summer afternoon in Virginia, 1863. All about me went out of focus except for the two young men, the road, and me.

"Good afternoon gentlemen," came the voice from me as natural as water. "Been hunting?"

"Yes ma'am," Mr. B. offered politely.

"Haven't had much luck?"

"No ma'am," W.T. spoke. I looked at his face. It was so familiar. He looked back at me with what seemed to be a similar emotion. "But we do have a few hours of daylight remaining." The genteel drawl added softness to the moment. I smiled broadly with my secret and deep love for this handsome young man whom I knew so well from his writing, and who now I could see face to face. The two men looked at each other, and then back at me.

"Do you live around here?" W.T. asked.

"Why no, I don't." I knew I could not fake an accent from another time, another place. "Just visiting. But my affections are with Virginia." They seemed somewhat relieved.

"Are you in need of help?" he offered, sensing my foreignness. I was touched at his kindness. His manners were thoroughly engrained

"No, thank you, sir. I'm on a mission. Are you gentlemen hungry?"

They exchanged glances again, and with a disarming smile W.T. answered, "Well ma'am, there is a war going on. But we are doing better than most."

"Oh, you are well brought up, I can tell, but I know hungry men when I see them. I have a basket here I would like for you to have."

There was a pause as they looked at the brimming basket covered with a cloth.

"Well that is mighty kind, but we could not take your basket of food from you."

"I would be honored to provide some food for soldiers from the Army of Northern Virginia."

"You are very generous, but we simply could not," Mr. B. joined the refusal.

"Oh, I insist."

"No thank you ma'am," W.T. interrupted. "You are clearly on your way to help someone, and I am sure there are those with greater need." He was so thoroughly Southern, and I loved him, a precious young man caught up in mannerliness and virtue for which he was willing to die. But I had the upper hand. I understood the game of southern manners. I set the basket at their feet.

"Please, my good soldiers, take this food and enjoy it. When I left this afternoon for my walk, I'm quite sure the Good Lord told me to pack a basket of food for someone who would need it. And I'm quite sure the two of you are that someone. It is not really from me. It is from His hand. So you cannot refuse."

They were speechless. They looked down at the basket and back at me. My eyes twinkled with the delight of out-mannering gentlemen of the Old South.

"May the Good Lord bless you and keep you safe in all these troubles." It was a prayer I had prayed over him many times.

"Thank you so very much." W.T. took my hand in his and looked me one more time in the eyes with that same puzzled look of *don't-I-know-you?* He kissed my hand. I curtsied, the best I was able without proper training. They picked up the basket and watched me walk on down the road. I turned to wave. They saluted smartly and then turned to go.

I heard W.T. say to his companion when he thought I was out of earshot, "She is most certainly not from around these parts."

Nancy Larner

TRAYNE 1827

Born Trayne, a name traced from our biblical mother Esther, my parents call me Ray. Ray, a ray of sunshine? That would be welcomed, but at fourteen my life, so far, has been no ray of sunshine, rather quite gloomy and very difficult. As a family, we barely get enough to eat. I am at an age when Tatah, my papa, could foreseeably start thinking of a match for me. But who would want this skinny bag-of-bones dressed in torn, mended and re-mended clothes? Frankly, there is no one in this village I would want as a husband so, *Oif morgen zal Got zorgen.* Let God worry about tomorrow.

It is difficult to keep warm during these long, winter days. We all huddle as close to the woodstove as possible and wear as much clothing as we can. The younger children often stay in bed and play under their blankets for warmth, but the wind's cold breath exhales frigid rivulets through spaces between the wood slats and freezes our feet numb.

Momeh reluctantly asks me to buy *Shabbos* candles, something she forgot on market day. Bundled against a snowstorm, I set out on my mission to Meyerwitz's Supply Store. Drifts are piling up against the houses. Each looks like an elder from *schul* with a long, flowing, white beard. A few kopeks in my pocket to accomplish the task, I knock, then enter the doorway so low that I, only fourteen, have to duck my head to enter. It takes a moment for my eyes to adjust to the gloom. On this dark day only a poor, hazy light comes through the small front and side windows. This store, like many others in our village, is a partitioned area in the front room of the family home. It is a dismal affair accentuated by the soot-stained, low-slung ceiling and wall behind the woodstove. A few bars of soap lie suffocating in a dusty wooden box. Stacked on sagging shelves sit soup kettles and bake pans. Hinges, locks, matches, and white memorial *yahrzeit* and *Shabbos* candles lay next to tallow candles for everyday use.

"Hello," I call out, "anyone here?"

Mrs. Meyerwitz, a short, plump roll of a woman makes her way from the curtained back room. "Oy," she puzzles, "who's this?" A toothless question forming, "An apparition? Who goes out on such a day?"

I laugh and pull my snow-covered *babushka* off my head and unwrap the brown, woolen scarf from around my mouth.

"It's me, Trayne! Momeh sent me for *Shabbos* candles."

"Trayne, out on such a day? I didn't recognize you so wrapped up. I thought maybe it was a snow *Gollum*," she giggles. "Oh, my dear, have you heard about the newest insult to Jews?" Going on before I could answer, "As if our lives aren't hard enough. Every day a struggle to survive. There is now a new tax on kosher meat and *Shabbos* candles. They do everything to make our lives a misery."

I reach into my pocket and hold my palm under her squinting eyes.

"This is all I have."

"Dear, it's not enough."

I drop my chin to my chest mumbling, "Momeh doesn't like to owe anyone."

Mrs. Meyerwitz reaches up to smooth my dark, wavy hair that falls below my shoulders, drying with her hand what is now wet from melting snow, "Take the candles." She grasps the pure white tapers awkwardly with an arthritic hand. "Tonight is *Shabbos*, you must have them. Momeh can make up the difference later, with a *challah* or a nice loaf of dark rye." She presses the candles into my hand. "Go, get home before you freeze."

I shiver as I step back outside after spending ten minutes with Mrs. Meyerwitz in her dingy but warm front room, my precious purchase tucked under my shawl. The snow swirling around me quickly covers my tattered clothing with a fresh layer of white. I smile to myself, pretending to be Queen Esther, my namesake, dressed in a glorious ball gown for the sumptuous banquet I am hosting for my King Ahasueros. I lite through the narrow streets. Snow-sparkles twirl around me, giving me courage to expose Haman's evil plan to kill the Jews of *Shoshan* told in the *Purim* story.

As night falls, our family gathers around Momeh who lights the *Shabbos* candles and recites the blessing with a waver in her voice. I know she is worried about owing, but the candlelight shining on Momeh, Tatah, Shimmel, Itzik and me makes us feel we have the warmest, coziest home in all of Ruzhany.

CROSSING

Dampness fills my nostrils, I smell a heavy pungency from the river as we near. The moon fractures into tiny flashes floating on the water, reminding me of the gleeful sparks that fly around inside our woodstove when Tatah, Papa, lays on a fresh log. Oh how they dance, wanting to bring joy and warming comfort to all of us in our spacious kitchen... I choke back a sob, remembering where I am.

In the pale light, I barely detect a dark figure sitting hunched over in a small wooden skiff. He seems to be sleeping, but as soon as we make our way through the dense, low brush onto the muddy river bank, he shoots straight up.

"Who's there?" a gruff voice booms, clearly annoyed at having been startled.

"Who's that?" I whisper to Zelig.

"Shhhh, let me do the talking."

Zelig asks this questionable figure if we can hire him to take us across.

"You'll have to pay me now. It's over an hour's worth of hard rowing in this swift current."

Zelig holds out two rubles. The man snatches the money greedily and shoves it into some secret place under his shabby wool cloak. We remove our shoes. Zelig holds the boat steady as Mirel and I take our place in the stern. Zelig sits one seat closer to the sinister-looking oarsman. In the dim moonlight his deep-set, dark eyes look empty, hidden under shaggy eyebrow awnings. Surrounded by an unkempt beard, his thin lips perpetually sneer. A shiver runs through me and I huddle closer to my eight-year-old sister for warmth and comfort. Although exhausted from walking most of the night, she sits poker-straight and will not remove her wide-eyed stare from the ominous figure to whom we have entrusted our safety. We set off. Leaning on Mirel and lulled by waves rhythmically slapping the side of the skiff, all is quiet. I doze.

"Stop that," Zelig demands.

I startle awake. The boat is rocking violently. Mirel swallows a cry. Her eyes spill over with fear. The man has stopped rowing and is thrusting his body from side to side, causing the craft to lurch this way and that, smacking the surface of the water. Mirel and I hold on to the gunnels and each other with all of our strength. The boatman has placed the paddle end of the oars on the inside of the skiff while he rocks, trying furiously to knock us into the water. Zelig, with one quick pull, yanks an oar from its lock, stands and pushes the handle end hard into the man's neck, forcing him to choke as his head is forced backward.

"Stop that, I said," Zelig growls again. "I'm not afraid to use this thing. Then we'll row ourselves across."

The man stops rocking, curses under his breath, takes the oar from Zelig, and continues rowing. It would have been more lucrative for him to dispose of us where the river is deepest, go back to shore, and pick up another unsuspecting party of Jews trying to escape the Cossacks. When found, our dead bodies would not have caused suspicion — just more poor souls trying to escape by swimming this swift-moving river. Luckily our older brother is wise to this kind of trouble.

An orange finger of light is just beginning to show itself on the eastern horizon when we, once again, thankfully feel dry land. A small shed filled with fishing nets doubles as a bed for a few hours. Another night has passed, and we, are still alive.

Eleanor Lowrey

JACK LEAVES US

My world breaks apart a day in March 1951. Though I no longer remember the date, the day is strong in my mind. It's when Jack, a U.S. Army doctor on the way to the Korean War, leaves my daughters and me in Hecla, South Dakota, with my parents.

We are living in Maryland while Jack attends a class at Walter Reed, the famed Army hospital, when he gets his orders to Korea. The following days are all about Jack's leaving us. I write to my parents and tell them about his orders. They write back and tell me the girls and I will live with them while he is in Korea. We move in with them shortly before Jack leaves us.

Before that really happens, I imagine different scenarios of the dreaded moment when he actually steps away from me. In one, I take him to the train. We stand by the huffing, puffing black giant and hold hands until the conductor calls "All aboard." Then, we lightheartedly say goodbye using as little emotion as we spend each morning when he goes to the hospital. It's a denial plan.

In another, *Poof!* I don't see him step on the train, it leaves, the train filled with noisy soldiers carries my husband to war, leaves but I don't know if he is on the train. I hunt for him, and finally he writes from Korea, telling me he is there. It's a goofy mystery plan, one I hope doesn't happen.

In another, the children stay with my parents while he and I go to the train in Aberdeen, the large city near Hecla, and I return to my parents and children after a day of shopping. A quick and dirty plan, it is the one we intend to use, but we don't because a sudden need to be alone with Jack and without our children or my parents overtakes me.

Driven, I hunt for Mama, find her in the kitchen, and without anyone else nearby I ask, "May I leave the children with you while I take Jack to the train?"

"Oh, yes. Leave when you want."

"I'd like to go today, though Jack won't board the train until tomorrow morning. May we do that?"

"Do what you need to do, Eleanor."

Elated, I find Jack. "Instead of taking you to the train in the morning, I am going to take you to the train as soon as you are packed. We'll spend the night at the hotel. In the morning, I'll walk to the depot with you and you'll board the train after our short walk from the hotel. I'll walk back alone, pack, check out, and shop. Then I'll drive to Hecla and arrive in the afternoon before Sue gets home from school."

Quickly he stashes his few personal items in his long, khaki-colored canvas bag, sweeps through the house looking for any other thing he might want with him, hugs, kisses, and says "Goodbye" to my parents and our two youngest daughters, puts his bag on the back seat of our maroon four-door Plymouth, and gets in the driver's seat.

I am already in the passenger seat when Jack steps into the car, expecting to wait for me. Surprised, he smiles and quickly starts the car, taking the short route to Aberdeen through the dimming light of this March day. We finish the last few miles of the fifty-mile ride to Aberdeen in the darkness of a moonless night.

Bathed in unspoken, forbidding lonesomeness, we register at the hotel, eat a light supper in the nearly empty coffee shop, enter our floor number on the new-fangled elevator, step off it at our floor, and, as though we are heading to the gallows, move our feet heavily and slowly down a long, dimly lit hallway and into our room.

In that short, dreaded night, we snuggle. We don't move away from each other and we don't talk. All there is to feel has been felt; all there is to say has been said. Jack has to leave and Susan, Gretchen, Georgia, and I have to spend our lives without him.

This is wartime living, and I know there is nothing we can do to prevent Jack's leaving. We are helpless. In the dark of the early morning the harsh ring of the hotel's alarm clock signals it is train time.

Jack gets up, shaves, and dresses while I stay in bed.

He asks, "Are you ready?"

"No. I can't walk with you. I did plan to do that, Jack, but I have changed my mind. We will have to say our goodbyes here."

Wearing my long nightgown, I go to open the bedroom door and stop. Jack steps through it and turns toward me. Voicelessly, he looks at me and I at him. He wears his full length, drab woolen coat. Its brass buttons, major's leaf, and caduceus glitter against the olive. His shoes are polished and his stiff hat sits comfortably on his head. I see an Army major; I don't see my husband.

His uniform stands between us. Yet, we kiss goodbye again and again, murmuring, "I love you with each kiss." How many kisses? How many goodbyes? How many I-love-yous? I don't know. They come until the train's jarring whistle separates us, saying, "Your time is up."

It is now time for him to leave me, time for him to walk alone to the Milwaukee Railroad Station, time for him to go to war, time for both of us to wonder if we'll be a family again.

Quickly Jack turns his back to me and walks to the elevators. He does not look back. His khaki duffle bag hanging over his left shoulder is the monkey on his back. I move into the hallway and focus my eyes in the direction he takes, hoping he will come back for just one more kiss.

He doesn't.

A soldier on active duty, he now is all business and I am a lonesome Army wife, looking down a dark hotel hallway in Aberdeen, South Dakota, in the direction my husband, an Army doctor, a major, walks. I do not move until I hear the clang of the automatic elevator door and know he is gone.

Empty, I step back into our room. I plan to shop during the morning, but going from store to store no longer tempts me. Instead, I hurriedly dress and leave the hotel. The need to be back in Hecla, back with my daughters and my parents, pushes me out of Aberdeen.

Harkening to the Bible's "There is a time to..." I drive slowly. Mile after mile, I spread out the jangled mess of feelings and reflections within me, look at each, think about it, and keep driving into the rising sun. As the miles disappear in the early morning light, the routines of others' lives show in the lighted windows of the spare prairie farmhouses I pass.

They bring it to me: their lives are not the ones changing. Mine is. It is time for me to face my new reality. I am alone. I am in charge of our children. Making decisions about them is mine to do, mine alone. They are not my parents' responsibility.

I repeat it again and again, stopping only when I am sure I've got it: *I alone am in charge.*

When I come into Hecla, I go straight to Mama's and Daddy's, turning onto the little road along the front yard. Gretchen, who is playing by herself, sees me. In a rapid, jarring sequence, she runs to the car's open door, steps on the running board, looks inside, turns her face to me, and asks, "Where is Daddy?'

"He's gone to war."

"Oh."

Somehow her dismissive yet accepting "Oh" comforts me. Gretchen can't understand what it means, but knowing as much as I tell her satisfies her and is insightful to me. The days ahead for us will be bad and good, depending on how I handle incidents such as this one.

I step out of the car and pick her up. I can't yet speak. I can't talk about what our move to Hecla and her father's leaving means to her, to her two sisters, and to me. I can't voice the cramping fears churning inside me. I can't put words to my turmoil, but I can hug her. And I do.

Wordless, I put her down and take her hand. We walk through the back door of my parents' house and step into Mama's bright yellow kitchen, where the tea kettle whistles, "Welcome."

I shut the door behind us and smile. We are home.

Hildegard Maas

RUSSIAN INVASION – 1945

The Russian Army was moving from the east into Pomeranian Germany. The city just east of our town was taken the day before. Luckily for us, my father had moved my children and me to the safety of my old hometown, Kordeshagen. After many months of relentless bombing by the Allies, Germans had been fleeing *from* western Germany to the safety of the east – but now we started seeing people walking west. There were no trains available because the German army had confiscated them long before. All the roads were blocked with people trying to get back to the west – away from the rapidly advancing army.

The nearby resort harbor city of Kolberg was inundated with refugees – thousands of people heading back west since the Russians were now conquering eastern Germany. Recent evacuees had been told by the German army that they could board ships in the harbor and be taken to "safety" – but no actual destination was mentioned. The small group of German soldiers who had been left to protect the city was unable to: we were all too aware of a ship loaded with 400 children for transport which had been bombed – and that there were no survivors.

Since our town was a county seat, the Nazis had made it a command post, but had suddenly departed with all of their weapons and supplies. The town elders now went out to face the Russian army coming in from the east, hoping there would be a peaceful takeover of our town. The Russians were anxious to meet their western Allies for the final blow to Germany, so they moved into our town and quickly took over...but hardly peacefully.

The next morning a Russian commander ordered all women of around twenty-five years old to bring a shovel and report for a march to the beaches of the Baltic Sea – closely guarded by soldiers. When we arrived we were surprised when we were told to dig holes in the sand until told to stop. We wondered why because we thought the war was over. At the end of the day, we were exhausted but saw many Russian soldiers watching us – waiting for us to finish, and we were scared. Once dismissed, we ran terrified through the fields making our way home...but knew they had ordered us to appear the next day for the same work at the beach. Then coming home the following day, we learned the terrible news: more than 200 of the men in our town had been taken away by the Russian army. These were the town elders, teachers, our doctor, merchants, husbands...and my own father. No one was told why, or where they had been taken. The third morning, everyone else in the town was ordered to gather our belongings and leave. Now we knew the war was *not* over.

For some time the only help we had left on the farm was one of the war prisoners, routinely used for hard labor. My husband was of French origin and during the times he could come home from serving in the German army, he had befriended one of the farmhands – a Frenchman himself. I had watched as they forged some sort of plan or understanding, something that my husband would not tell me about...for my own safety, he would say. Fortunately, this Frenchman took control of our hasty departure: telling us what to pack, what to leave, and where to go. We left, with our meager possessions and only transportation: two horses and a cart.

We walked all day to a town south of us – occupied by the Russian army. We discovered that there were others from our former town already there, and were told we could bed down in a stable, which we did and were thankful to have that. Our luck ran out the next morning when the French prisoner (and by then our dear friend and protector) was taken away, under the pretense that he would be reunited with others from his country. We were devastated to be separated – we had become like family and had grown to rely on and care for each other. All our lives had changed again...

A Russian Commander witnessed our tearful goodbyes to our French friend, obviously struck by our friendship and sadness at parting. He informed us we must again depart, this time for a "quiet town near the woods" approximately three hours away. We saw many things on our way, but one gruesome and unbelievable sight I unfortunately cannot forget. We came across the bodies of two adult women, sisters as it turned out, and three children. We learned of their tragic story by reading the letter left by one of the women: She explained that the rock-covered grave nearby was her sister who had killed herself – out of grief, despair, or simply not being able to go on. After burying her, the remaining sister slit the wrists of the three children...then did the same to herself, bleeding out there in the woods. We believed she probably felt the same hopelessness and desperation that her sister, and so many others, felt.

We walked on for hours, finally coming to a town that was seemingly quiet and with the only evidence of Russian occupation being soldiers resting and preparing for what lay ahead. We were thrilled when an officer told us we could move into one of the many deserted homes in town. We stayed about two weeks, trying to ignore the outside world as much as we could – wanting to bring some normalcy to our lives. One day, children from the town were playing in the nearby woods but came running home, shouting that "There's a man in the woods and he's asking if the Vanselow family is here!" Knowing it *must* be my father, my mother took off running to find him. But when he saw her coming towards him he told her to stop. It seems he was covered with any number of disgusting materials: dirt, sweat, lice, animal waste...and more. She convinced him to take his clothes off for her to clean – because they had nothing else for him to wear. Then, not having any other option, my mother took these flea and lice-ridden garments and put them in the outdoor oven – our only means of disinfecting them.

Over the next days, sympathetic townspeople helped my father recover from his severe fatigue, malnutrition, and mental shock. They brought food and other simple items of comfort, which they thought might help revive him. But after a short time, curiosity got the best of the townsfolk, and they begged him for information about his experiences and news from where he had been.

Reluctantly, he related the story of what happened to him and the other 200 men who were taken. He said that before making it even to the next town, *ten* of those men were killed – many shot simply because they could no longer go on. Many had served in WWI, so due to old age or injuries they were unable to keep up with the younger men in the group. We heard my father go on to explain much of what had happened during those four weeks with the men from his town. We didn't want to hear, but had to listen.

The men were eventually taken to a work camp of some kind, but he didn't know where they were. The men were sick and weak, and the work was strenuous. Survivors were slowly being killed or dying from inhumane treatment, disease, starvation, or suicide. One day a Russian soldier called my father aside to "do a job for him"...but my father said he had the feeling that this guard was giving him a rare chance to escape. This soldier spoke some German and my father believed this Russian felt some empathy for his prisoners. So, my father simply walked away when he saw his chance, disappearing into the nearby woods. By the time he escaped, my father was one of only *twelve* men who survived this horrendous ordeal.

This is the story of only one of thousands... thousands of women and men who lived the horrors of this time.

Peggy Markham

MUD

Minnie Clair Myers Reeves was my great-grandmother. We called her "Mud." She was born in 1872 and died in 1959. She lived her entire life in the Low Country of South Carolina. This is an incident I recall on a visit to see Mud. I was seven years old.

Mud's bedroom reeks of rosewater, liniment, and the stale scent of an old woman. The window shades hang limp, drawn down for protection against the August sun's harsh intrusion. No breeze filters the still air. I stand at the foot of her brass bed beside my mother and my grandmother.

Mud stirs beneath a faded quilt and pushes herself up to a sitting position buffered by soft, down pillows. Her child-like frame is draped in an ecru nightgown made of sheer linen and embroidered with dainty flowers. Covering her head is a sleeping cap of pale pink silk adorned in tiny ribbon rosettes. Wisps of curly, gray hair slip out of the braids tucked beneath the cap.

Like a cat awaking from a nap, she blinks her eyes, annoyed by the slivers of sunlight seeping into the room behind the drawn shades. From under the coverlet her hands, like papery thin bird claws, scratch out searching for her fan. The fan is an old church fan made of stiff cardboard glued to a popsicle stick. On the front of the fan is a picture of Jesus wearing a purple robe with white lilies strewn around his bare feet. Mud waves the fan in the soiled air.

My mother shoves me forward as she announces in a rather loud voice, "Mud, this is your great-granddaughter, Margaret Rose." Whispering in my ear my mother instructs me to say something nice. I think Mother believes that Mud is deaf. I yank my sundress with nervous, damp hands and pipe, "Mud, are you crazy? Mama and Grandmama say you're as crazy as a June bug!"

Mud's doll-like head swivels around towards me and my mother and she gives us a look that would melt magnolia blossoms off the tree. The room thrums with the croon of locusts hiding in the jasmine bush outside the bedroom window. The sun beats against the drawn shades. Nothing stirs in the dead air.

My mother hooks her fingers on my arm and leads me out of the room.

LOST IN PARADISE

In the chain of Hawaiian islands is the island of Oahu, lush in greenery, washed fresh by gentle rain showers and graced with beaches of crystal white sand. Clouds pillow the blue sky and the sea whispers in waves of rolling surf. Palm trees riffle in the perfumed breezes. Plumeria flowers and *pikake* leaves strung into ropey leis drape the shoulders of visitors. Honolulu, Hawaii... paradise. It was like that in 1965.

******

Kui Lee sang, "I'll remember you, your sweet laughter, mornings after, I'll remember you." He shifted the lyrics easily from English to his native Hawaiian. The moon slid over Diamond Head and hushed waves broached the beach of Waikiki.

We had gathered for a luau at the Princess Kaiulani Hotel. Our group consisted of young married couples. The men were officers, pilots in the Air Force, stationed at Hickam Field. Newcomers to the island, fresh from the Mainland, we were delighted with the rotation to Hawaii. To be based in Honolulu was a highly-sought-out assignment in the military.

A breeze rippled in from the ocean brushing the palm trees surrounding the lanai of the hotel. We ate island fare of *pupus* (hors d'oeuvres) and drank the tropical favorite Mai Tai rum drink adorned with a tiny paper umbrella stuck in a floating pineapple ring. As part of the evening's entertainment, Hawaiian musicians dressed in floral shirts strummed ukuleles and sang native songs. Slender girls with long, dark hair and swaying grass skirts danced the hula.

One pretty *wahine* pulled my husband, David, on to the dance floor and with a sense of fun encouraged him to hula with her. His embarrassment showed in his awkwardness of uneven hip swings. We cheered him on and soon the other men joined the dancers. A brace of starched khaki uniforms among the supple grass skirts.....an evening of innocence, of playing in paradise.

Far away to the west across the vast Pacific Ocean a treacherous storm was stalking us, bearing down with ferocious intensity. The storm roiled in a small Asian country where a civil war raged. We would soon become familiar with that country's name, Vietnam. A greedy jungle lying in wait for the innocents.

Under the mango tree,
lies rotted fruit.
Bite the mango.
Too sweet. Too ripe.

******

In less than a year after our arrival, more and more military personnel flooded Oahu. Navy ships, Marines in Kaneohe, airplanes constantly arriving and leaving Hickam Field. David's flying missions increased with long flights staging across the Pacific through Guam, Wake, the Philippines, Japan, Thailand, Vietnam. His plane was a bulky monster, a huge C-124 cargo aircraft, used to ferry supplies and troops to Vietnam. His plane picked up soldiers in Saigon and brought them to Hawaii for R & R (rest and relaxation) or he transported fresh troops to Da Nang Air Base in Vietnam. David said the soldiers on their way over were raucous and full of energy but the men he flew home were quieter. They would file on board the plane and slump down into their seats with very little chatter among them. A despondent silence.

I was busy caring for two babies and I felt protected and insular on the military base, going to the beach, lunching with the other wives at the officer's club. We knew there was a terrible storm swirling around us but we simply carried on with daily routines. Living in paradise among sweet flowers, surrounded by the gentle, sighing sea was a life of innocent illusion.

The flight crews often brought home items purchased in the foreign places where they had lay-overs. From Japan were the BBQ hibachi pots which looked like giant green eggs, teakwood furniture from the Philippines, brassware and precious jewels from Bangkok.

One day, as David prepared to leave for Saigon, a trip that would take two weeks, I asked if when he was in Bangkok could he buy a princess ring or a jewel, like an emerald or a ruby.

"All my friends are getting them and they are so beautiful," I said. It seemed a casual request.

"Sure," he responded, "we should have a lay-over there for a day or two."

The day he came home from that trip I felt there was something different about him. He looked very tired, weary and depleted. Usually, he was so happy to be home, finished with the mission, ready to relax back into our family's routine. He unpacked his gear bag of grease-stained flying suits, dirty laundry, unpolished boots, dog-eared flight manuals.

I asked nonchalantly, "Did you buy a ring or emerald in Bangkok?"

David uttered a long, heavy sigh. "No, we didn't stop in Thailand. We went straight to Saigon. We didn't bring back rings or BBQ pots, no brassware, no stuff. Our cargo was only coffins. Caskets. So many caskets wrapped in American flags. Dead soldiers. Lots of dead Marines."

I never got a princess ring nor did I ever ask for one again. David did bring an emerald stone from Bangkok on his last flight to Thailand before we rotated back to the Mainland. We had it set into a ring that I wear every day. It is a reminder that life is more precious than any jewel.

1966 – Southeast Asia. Saigon. Vietnam. Ho Chi Minh. Hanoi.
Viet Cong. Black pajamas, camouflage jackets,
slanted eyes, round eyes,
rickshaws, helicopters,
bird song in the jungle, napalm in scorched trees,
fried shrimp on a kabob, roasted babies in rice paddies,
princess rings with rubies, dog tags on white crosses.

Paradise found. Paradise lost.

Laura Mehmert

THE QUILT

I sit in front of my window at my sewing machine pinning the colorful fabric, guiding it carefully under the needle. Reds blues yellows greens, a cacophony of patterns and designs. The squares become rows, the rows eventually become your quilt top. The pleasant smell of fabric starch and warm cotton fills my nose as I slowly iron the seams, thinking of you, thinking of our times together. This is good fabric tightly woven, made to last for years, years you no longer have.

I wonder if you're sitting on your front porch this morning drinking coffee and watching the deer graze. You told me you often sit in the white rocker and watch the deer silently steal across your lawn at dawn.

I finished your quilt this morning, wrapped it in plain white tissue. I told you I was sending you greeting cards so you'll be surprised to receive a large box. I hope it will make you smile.

You called tonight after you received your quilt. You've been crying since it arrived, overwhelmed at the meaning of this gift that was made especially for you. I tell you that each stitch carries a prayer for your well being, for your survival. You will take it to chemo next week, drape it over your lap, wrap yourself in my love.

REGGIE

When I was about eight years old, our family decided to get a second dog. Our first dog being sweet little Lassie, a red, freckle-faced cocker spaniel about four years old. We eagerly scanned the classified ads and found one that looked hopeful. One-year-old boxer, "Free to Good Home." We called and made arrangements to meet the pooch the following weekend. For some reason, I envisioned a sweet little black and white Boston Terrier type dog. What we *got* was a fifty-five pound hunk of muscle and personality named "Reggie." His owner was a police officer who couldn't spend enough time with such a high-energy dog. We were thrilled to welcome him into our family unit.

He was a golden tan black-muzzled dog with a white patch on his chest and paws, an altogether handsome specimen soon to be known for his daring and bravery. He arrived with a few traits that needed work. He had the bad habit of cornering any tardy student walking to school. He would block their path and growl at them until they dropped their sack lunch. He then would daintily retrieve his prize, trot away with the lunch, and gulp it down...paper and all. He also *bit* everyone in the family and several of our neighbor children. The only one who escaped his teeth was Mom. She was the wielder of the lawn mower, the *only* thing that frightened fearless Reggie.

My brother John would come running up to the back door yelling, "Mom! Get the lawn mower! Reggie's got a hold of Bonnie Loesche!" (Reggie was not one to bite and let go. He would bite and *hold* on, a Boxer trait, I've learned.) Mom would head for the garage, crank up the mower and wend her way across the back yard...mowing a swath through the yard, right through the narrow gate and the Joyce's yard, then on to the screams emanating from the Loesches. You could almost hear the trumpets heralding her arrival! In about ten minutes, here they'd come: Mom and the lawn mower, with John holding a repentant Reggie by the collar.

We grew to love our rugged charge. We taught him how to sit and stay. We would drape a slice of Kraft cheese over his nose and he would form long strings of drool and tremble until we said, "Okay, Reggie, you can have it!" His favorite was baloney. We even entrusted Joanne, our fragile green parakeet, to him. She wobbled and pecked her way across his broad brow as we rolled on the floor, shrieking with laughter! He seemed to know it wouldn't be right to gobble her down. He did eat the occasional pot roast off the counter, prompting Mother to put dinner at the back corner of the stove with the heavy aluminum roasting pan in front to keep it from his ready jaws. He was pretty handy getting hamburgers off the grill as well.

One day I heard Reggie barking in the back yard. My Grandma Sea ran out and saw a meter reader wildly swinging his metal tape measure in a large twelve-foot arc over his head! Each time it passed Reggie, he would zoom in for a nip. Grandma said, "Young man, *what* did you *do* to that dog?" The sweating man replied, "Lady, I'm just here to read the meter. *Please* call *off* your dog!"

We loved that he was such a loyal watchdog. His deep growl could raise the hair on the back of your neck and send any salesman packing. We never worried when we were home alone. No one could get past him. Once my dad came home after midnight and didn't realize Reggie was on the front porch. Without so much as a growl, Reggie had his feet on Dad's shoulders and his jaws around his neck as Dad squeaked out, "Reggie, it's me." Dad gained a new respect for him in that moment.

Our neighbors, the Conrads, bred little Dachshunds. Nothing made Reggie happier than sailing over the fence, racing madly around in circles, getting them all riled up to chase him, then flying back over the hedge into our yard before the neighbor could get his shoes laced up and get out the door. A perverse delight for our Reggie and an unending source of pride to my brothers and me!

He was famous for fighting all dogs that appeared to be a threat. This never included small dogs. That was beneath him. However the cast of *big dogs* was legend. He carried the scars to prove it. Many years later he would take on Lash, the Malamute and neighborhood bully, who was twice his size, and the wounds he received in that fight would lead to his eventual death, a warrior to the end.

During the school year I'd get called out of class to the front office and Mrs. Williams would say, "Laura, your dog is out on the playground. Go get him and take him home." I'd go out to find Reggie humping some poor child's leg. I would drag him off, apologize to the embarrassed student, and walk my buddy home. Chattering to him all the way, loving that he was *mine*!

In the summer, we'd let Reggie take naps with us on the twin beds in the North Room. We named rooms for either their position in the house or the wallpaper that graced their walls. Mom did not approve of a dog or dog *hairs* on a bed. We finally just unlatched the window screen and when we heard her coming we just shoved him out the window. It was a good five-foot drop to the ground. He never seemed to complain. Mom ignored the hairs and paw prints. He adored us and we adored him. Any time spent together was the *high* life!

Looking back over our happy years with Reggie, I've come to realize he was my first confidant. Many hours were spent on the back porch sitting next to Reggie, whispering secrets into his soft fur. Telling him of some slight or perceived injustice. His soulful brown eyes always seeming to understand. He would lean into my shoulder offering his broad body as a brace, my friend forever. He was always game for any adventure, be it a walk in the woods, a ball toss, or perusing the refrigerator for last night's leftovers. I dream of him, at times, of being in peril, and I call out to Reggie. I awaken with the certain knowledge that, could he slip the bounds of Heaven, he'd be at my side.

Because of our wonderful experiences, I have found myself embracing many more four-legged friends over the years. All shapes, all sizes, all breeds. Each in their own way have carved a special niche into my heart and enriched my life beyond measure. They continue to amaze, delight, and warm my soul. To think, it all started with Reggie.

PEONIES

Cora-Cedar Hill Cemetery is surrounded by a white picket fence and dotted with large handsome cedar trees. I wander through this centuries-old cemetery viewing the various headstones. Some are crumbled and unreadable, others dark and covered with lichen, some looking almost new. Lovely peony bushes of white, pink, and fuchsia are scattered throughout, a testament to the hardiness of the bush and the pioneers who planted them. Purple and yellow iris salute the morning sun. A stand of Shasta daisies sway in the wind.

I stop at an exceptionally fine peony bush, bend to cup the velvet petals in my hands, crush my nose into the fuchsia center. So shameless in its beauty, standing watch behind Grandma's headstone with its large showy blossoms. Does it squander its life in this quiet spot off a dusty country road, seen only by the Memorial Day family members and the occasional new arrival? Or does it soothe visitor and resident alike, making us smile with its glorious show of color for the living as well as the dead?

Lynn Mergen

LITTLE BRIDES OF JESUS

When we were eight years old Charlene told me to expect a tingling throughout my entire body when I received Holy Communion the first time. At that moment, she confided... I would surely know the glory of God.

Anticipation was enormous, together with the angst of selecting the perfect white dress, veil, shoes and socks. Little brides of Jesus awaiting His consumption and the realization of being one with our Lord.

Much to my surprise, the only awareness I had after the host was placed on my tongue was...how do I get it off the roof of my mouth!

SHOPPING CART ETHICS

(Written to Father Mickiewicz, on September 8, 2005)

Dear Father Bill,

I'd like to tell you a story of a discussion I had with my grandson, Duncan, about the shopping cart which we (well....I) brought back from Singapore.

While shopping the other day for school clothes with Duncan, he saw someone pushing a shopping cart at the mall, and he remarked at how unusual it was to see someone at the mall with a shopping cart.

We discussed it for a while, musing that it would make sense at malls because people buy so much and have many bags to tote around.

Finally Duncan looked at me with his beautiful big eyes, and said, "Grandma, why do you have a shopping cart at your house?" (I have a shopping cart which I let the movers pack and bring back from Singapore.....our maid had used it to transport groceries to our apartment, and it was gold, able to turn on a dime, and smaller than the huge US carts.)

"It comes from a Singapore grocery store named Jason's Market," I said not really answering the question.

"Well did they give it to you, or did you forget you had it when you moved?" he asked, with wide eyes which said he knew the answer, but needed to hear it from me.

"I didn't forget I had it, and they didn't give it to me," I answered, realizing I had just confessed to stealing something to my seven-year-old grandson.

"I know, my mom and I figured it out," he said with those big eyes, and a hint of a smirk.

"Maybe I should write a letter and apologize to Jason's Market," I offered.

"Well, I think it's better to talk about it than to do nothing," he wisely said.

"I don't take things that don't belong to me, but I guess this clearly doesn't belong to me, and it was wrong to take it," I said with my tail between my legs.

Long silence while Duncan absorbed this, and I felt foolish. No more discussion (thank God).

I decided that this was a lesson on many levels. First, stealing is a harsh word, but clearly I took it, and it was wrong. I *did* come clean to Duncan. Second, maybe he will forgive me and realize that even grandmas are human and make bad decisions once in a while. Third, I admitted that what I did was wrong, which in my opinion was taking the high road instead of making up a story that wasn't accurate but would have saved my butt from embarrassment. Fourth, what the hell do I do with the basket now? It is full of hats in my entryway, and in full view when one enters the house. I thought of many possible things to do with it.....but for now, I will leave it there to remind me of my poor judgment.

For me it was a humbling lesson of ethics, morals, and just how smart and observant children are!

CLICKING OF THE BEADS

I recall with happiness the flurry of cleaning and baking as the house was being readied for Rosary. My grandmother lined chairs in rows, carefully placed her statue of Mary on the head table, and baked *kolaches* with prune centers.

When the doorbell rang on the day of Rosary, my cousins and I were banished to the back bedroom to play, since this devotion was not for children.

Finally, after the greetings, acceptance of flowers, and Grandma's group taking their seats and then kneeling, the monthly adoration began.

"Mmmmmmmful....gra...mmmm....Je-sus." How mesmerizing yet hilariously funny it seemed to me and my cousins, prepubescent creatures that we were. We had escaped our quarantine and began spying on the ladies. We ran up and down the hall watching from two vantage points. The kneeling chorus clicking and clacking their beads, and monotone-ing the prayers, sounded a bit scary, but the thrill of the spying made it a great adventure.

Not guilt but happiness remains today fifty-five years later. It is replaced by a proud and satisfying feeling, that I now possess and cherish my grandmother's statue of Mary.

Anita Nielsen

MY FIRST AMERICAN MEAL IN CHINATOWN

A pale moisture-filled sky welcomed us to New York City in the month of March in 1950. At last, no more wind-tossed angry ocean waves with creaking and cracking sounds coming out of the ship's belly, the "Ile de France."

After we cleared through Ellis Island, our friends, the Brunners were waiting to take us to Chinatown. As I was seasick for the duration of our voyage, existing only on tea, broth, and crackers, I was ready for my first meal in America.

Upon entering the cozy Chinatown Restaurant, located a few steps below street level, my mind was repeatedly assaulted with diverse images. There was indeed an exotic world, a culture I had only heard about from my grandfather. The atmosphere, so foreign to this new immigrant girl, captivated my imagination.

A frail, small-boned waiter greeted us at the door, introducing himself, I believe, as Mr. Wang. His golden skin glowed in the dimly lit room. Dark eyes hid behind wire-rimmed glasses. To my amazement, Mr. Wang wore his gray hair twisted into a very long braid, dangling over his colorful embroidered silk robe. The droopy mustache reached to touch his thin, gray-speckled beard. To complete his authentic Chinese style of dress, Mr. Wang wore a round black silk pill-box hat to cover his balding head. It was a picture forever etched in my memory.

Suddenly, we were escorted to our table, passing carved jade-colored jars and blue ceramic bowls displayed on black lacquered shelves.

The walls were painted vivid red, the color symbolizing happiness and good luck, according to the Chinese culture.

Faint strains of a lute-like instrument drifted on the air from somewhere behind a curtained-off room. Nodding, smiling and bowing, Mr. Wang took our order and with small shuffling steps disappeared into the kitchen.

As my eyes adjusted to the shadowy room, I peered at the hand-painted cone-shaped lanterns depicting country scenes of China, while a circle of light flooded each small table. With curiosity, I continued to gaze upon an ancient paper scroll, sketched in shades of black ink, illustrating a gnarled evergreen tree shielding a simple pavilion.

Within minutes, Mr. Wang set a steaming pot of Oolong tea in the center of the table, its heavy, smoky odor tickling my nose. The porcelain tea cups felt heavy compared to the ones used at home. I wondered what happened to the missing handles – were they left behind in China?

Snatches of conversation and hearty laughter sounded from the kitchen area beyond another curtained door. The aromas of combined ginger root, lemon, garlic, Chinese cabbages, and onions escaped the kitchen as these morsels were thrown into a steel wok, sizzling and hissing in the peanut oil, stirred to perfection.

The food was delivered quickly by Mr. Wang, steam escaping from underneath covered bowls in assorted sizes. I was hungry, anticipating devouring the delicious food, until to my horror and perhaps a little foreboding, this cuisine was too foreign to me. I was politely trying a small serving from each bowl; however, I avoided the white bean sprouts, as they reminded me of worms. I noticed that throughout the meal my plate was mostly stacked with rice, a familiar food product, followed by ample gulps of Chinatown's famous tea.

Each year, I recall my first American meal in Chinatown with its exotic flavor, as I plant pea pods, Bok Choy, and garlic in my garden, as the Oriental cuisine has become my favorite food.

STORKS STILL RETURN EACH SPRING TO MY SWISS HOMETOWN

Firmly planted against the base of the Swiss Jura Mountains with the vineyards climbing the southern slopes reaching the forest, you will find my one-thousand-and-fifteen-year-old hometown named Lengnau.

My repeated walk from home to school was only one-half mile long. It led me along a gravel country lane weaving its way through cherry and apple orchards and old farmsteads. The meadows were beautifully sprinkled with white daisies, and blue cornflowers edged around the golden wheat fields.

My long braids touched the top of my apron-covered school dress. I hated to wear the ugly stockings that I knitted from scratchy make-believe wool.

I adored our new teacher whose skin was flawless; according to gossip she supposedly took daily milk baths, but no one could prove it.

Recess was short and the classroom emptied quickly. We ran outside to take a peek through the barred school basement window at the village jail. There was no crime with the exception of having the town's drunk disturbing the peace with his over-exuberant yodeling, mostly out of tune. After sleeping off the alcoholic intake, he was released to go home, quite happy to escape the children's prying eyes.

There was never an excuse for us being late, as the massive metal bells of our sixteenth-century church would loudly proclaim each hour.

In the spring the white storks would return from Africa to build nests on top of the church steeple or on house rooftops. I watched in awe as these spectacular birds with their ten-and-a-half-foot outstretched wingspan circled above me.

One summer, horse-drawn wagons of gypsies arrived outside town. They camped along the Aare River in the shade of a grove of Lombardy poplar trees. To support themselves, the men fixed broken umbrellas and sharpened knives, and an elderly grandma was a palm reader.

The wooden domed wagons were adorned with large paintings of flowers in eye-popping colors of yellow, orange, red and blue. While the cool evening breezes carried the smoke of a dying campfire, a dark-eyed beauty in her multi-colored dress performed a spirited dance to the sounds of a violin player.

Children were warned not to venture too close to the gypsy camp as they would kidnap us, but our lives were not lived in fear.

Coming home from school, I had to cross the suspended iron bridge overlooking the railroad tracks. If I timed it just right and my friends were available, we danced and giggled as the smelly iron horse below us belched black smoke from its belly, covering us in soot and grime. Needless to say, my mother would be very upset with me.

It's been told, once you leave your hometown, you lose your place, you can never return. This is true as I visited many years later and the place I loved had changed. I felt sad, something was missing, and I was a stranger in my hometown.

The storks still return each spring but they now settle away from our town, moving closer to the river.

The trains seldom stop at our little railroad station, passing on to larger cities.

Some of my beloved open spaces have been built upon with townhouses and other structures, a sad reminder that years have marched on.

The church bell continues to ring out the familiar time schedule. Some people complain about them making too much noise.

Most of my classmates have relocated to new horizons.

My teachers and shopkeepers and relatives of that group are now resting in the cemetery.

Looking back, I am happy to recall a less complicated and slower-paced childhood.

Carolyn Seymour

THE POSTMAN DURING WWII

Our farewell embrace at the airport was embarrassingly lengthy. My husband, who had been assigned duty as a Japanese language officer after completing a rigorous eighteen months studying the language at Colorado University in Boulder, Colorado, was departing for the Pacific theatre.

My working mother had agreed that I should come live with her and my two working sisters while I awaited the birth of our first child. She had kindly insisted on accompanying me to the airport to send Alan on his way.

I insisted on watching the plane depart, hoping he might see me again from the plane window. I waved my umbrella vigorously, which resulted in drenching my mother and me from the pouring rain. This stupid action did help to relieve the tension. I don't think he saw us. Thankfully, my mother and I were very silent as I drove back to our apartment.

Three anxious weeks passed before his first letter arrived. From this time on the arrival of the postman was the crowning event of the day – whether it would be gloomy or tolerably satisfying. Alan's letters were artfully cheerful, reflective and informative as far as he could manage with the censoring rules in control. I always replied with three or four pages of hopefully cheerful chit chat and occasionally a photo of me showing my bulging belly with the precious life percolating there.

The postman became the focus of my life. He reflected my mood and noticed whether I had received an overseas letter or not. He had been in the army in World War I but he never shared any of his experiences. When Alan was on a mission aboard a ship, he shared my anxiety. When the letter arrived announcing a safe return, we shared a thankful sigh. This was the longest waiting time

I had ever experienced in my life, not only for a baby's arrival, but for the letters delivered by a kind gentle man in a Post Office uniform who understood my anxious moments.

When Sue was born, Alan's precious letter, welcoming her and praising me, was delayed for ten days. The postman suffered as much anxiety as we did. When the peace treaty was signed, he cheered along with us, as we realized that the day was finally approaching when our men would be coming home.

After six months of duty in Japan, Alan did get home safely. The meeting with his almost-year-old daughter was memorable, and the postman cheerfully participated as we introduced him to Alan. We thanked him for being the link during the war when family communications were so important and necessary to maintain our sanity. Now, I wish I had learned more about his earlier life in another war. Why was he so sympathetic toward me? I wish I could remember his name.

Mary Simonich

GUN-TOTING FLOOZY

I was curled up on the sofa looking at old photographs when suddenly I became fascinated with someone I had never seen before. Sitting on a split rail fence with one snakeskin cowboy boot on the bottom rail and the other on the second rung was a rugged cowpoke dressed in tight Levis and a big flannel plaid shirt holding in the left hand a black Stetson and in the right hand a lit corncob pipe.

"Who is that?" I exclaimed. My mom smiled and said, "That is Katie Kallesen, your great-aunt on my mother's side. She used to ride the rodeo circuit. She would leap on her horse bareback and ride him around the arena; then she would do cartwheels, headstands, and reverse splits while they were moving."

"Why is she wearing a gun holster with six-shooters?" I asked, totally mesmerized by now. "She was a sharpshooter and a trick shooter as well. She could outshoot most of the men," Mom said. *Wow, a real live Annie Oakley in the family!*

"At least no one made her stay in when she was a young girl and make her do embroidery," I muttered. "Probably not," Mom replied, "but she did win blue ribbons at the State Fair for her rhubarb pie." *Wow, Annie Oakley and Betty Crocker in one person. I wonder why no one ever mentioned her.*

"Well," added Mom, "she liked men."

"Don't stop now," I pleaded. But one glance at the steely look in my mother's eye, the pinched mouth, and the stoic chin, I knew I would learn no more; Katie and her men would remain a mystery.

High jinx on horseback
With cheering crowds and bright lights
Quieted her restless soul

Barbara Sternberg

SAILING TO THE NEW WORLD

And so it was that I arrived alone in Hoboken, New Jersey, one fine day in July of 1946. Slimmer than when I had embarked on the voyage almost a week before, seen off from Glascow by my mother, sister, and my fiancé, Eugene. Despite my best resolutions, I was horribly seasick. When I landed I was handed a note from someone at the British Information Services, where I was to work, which gave me the Manhattan address of accommodations that had been arranged for me.

The next few weeks were a feast of experiences unlike any before or since. My residential quarters were in a penthouse apartment belonging to the widow of a New York State Supreme Court judge. This was in the long-vanished Sheraton Hotel on Lexington Avenue. My hostess/landlady was drenched in grief but wonderfully gracious and hospitable. I was able to walk to work at the British Information Services (B. I. S.) offices on the 32nd floor of the central building of the stunning, brand-new Rockefeller Center. Although I knew not a soul in my new environment, I was fortunate in having congenial and friendly colleagues at work and began eagerly to explore Manhattan's fabulous resources.

In late August it was time for Eugene to arrive in the U.S. We spent the entire first night together just walking in Manhattan, eating freshly-roasted nuts, catching up on each other's lives, and marveling at our new world.[1]

---

[1] Sternberg, Barbara. "Through Windows of Poetry." Unpublished Manuscript 37-38

THE MISTRESS OF CEREMONIES

Nobody appointed her to this office, but ever since the day she arrived on a long-delayed flight from England (it got stuck in Iceland for two days) just before Christmas of 1951, my mother became the Mistress of Celebrations. Still jet-lagged and nauseated, she managed to bake small English mince pies and jam tarts the first afternoon she was with us, to serve a small Christmas party of friends and their children. By this time Eugene and I had two young children, Elizabeth (Liz) and Frances (Franki as a teenager, now Francesca). Granny lived with us for many years as our family grew, adding three more children: Patrick (Pat), John, and Jennifer (Jenny).

She thought up party themes and cake decorations for the birthday of each of the growing family of grandchildren and delightedly discovered new holidays to celebrate. Valentine's Day had been for lovers back in England, but here in America she discovered it was democratically available to every child, and to every grown-up too, with a love of sweet heart-shaped cakes and cookies, and an appreciation for a festive dinner table rich with Cupid motifs and lacy Victorian linens.

With the long, bitter history dividing England from Ireland, St. Patrick's Day over there was a day to be dreaded for potential bomb explosions and more troubles in Northern Ireland. How wonderful to discover that over here it was mainly another joyful party theme: suppers of soda bread and corned beef with cabbage, decorations of cardboard green leprechauns, the table centerpiece a living shamrock plant, and a finale of efforts at Irish jigs to records of Gaelic music. Memorial Day, Presidents' Day, Labor Day – these were all new opportunities for her to think up special outings, games, picnics, brunches or dinners.

I will never forget the July 4th celebration we planned with her the year she became a U.S. citizen – with a long guest list, wonderful home-baked food, lots of children milling around and a huge red, white, and blue cake sporting the Stars and Stripes. It had taken her quite a number of years to decide to become an American citizen. It happened after she returned from a visit to England one year. She said that two differences between the two countries had impressed her deeply. The first was how many more opportunities were available to older people here – to train, re-train, undertake new activities, travel, volunteer, join an infinite variety of groups. The second was the still profound, and limiting, reality of the class structure in Britain.

On Easter Sunday, being a devout and practicing Christian, Granny was off to early church services. But not before she had hidden neat clusters of chocolate eggs and other Easter candies – one for each child – for the children to harvest on their morning hunt. She was the one who helped the kids dye Easter eggs, decorate Christmas cookies, and choose their Halloween costumes for which she then bought patterns and materials to sew. I was profoundly grateful for that contribution. I only have to look at a sewing machine and it starts screwing up. I am a firm believer in the idea that some skills can happily skip a generation. My mother sewed. Two of my daughters sew. That's perfectly okay.

The celebration fever of course reached its highest pitch at Christmas time. My mother spearheaded the decoration of every possible inch of our home, encouraging each child to decorate their rooms. Egged on by her enthusiasm, we all shopped for gifts, helped with baking, and wrote Christmas cards before the great day. Our Christmas tree was almost overwhelmed by the piles of presents around it.

On Christmas Eve, after the children had finally gone to bed, my mother and Eugene and I performed the final ritual – filling the Christmas stockings. This was no simple feat of stuffing in a few trifles. Every item had to be wrapped in Christmas paper, there had to be balance in what they each received so all were happy, and there should be a mix of wanted things, fun things, and surprises. Adults of course had to have stockings too, and so we stuffed eight stockings routinely, plus extras if guests happened to be staying.

I loved the hectic bustle, the outbursts of color, sounds, and activities on so many festive occasions each year, and the excitement of the children. But I must confess – it was lucky for me that I had a resident Mistress of Celebrations. I always did my part: shopping, baking, supervising games, clearing up. But I think being good at celebrations can be another generation-skipping skill. I am content now to lie in bed a little longer on Christmas mornings knowing my children's families are up at the crack of dawn – opening stockings, their mothers trying to get breakfast down young throats before the long-awaited task of unwrapping presents. I have found that what I truly celebrate are the ordinary things in life – the miracles of everydayness, the resumption of precious pedestrian activities after the festivities are over.[2]

---

[2] Sternberg, Barbara. "*Through Windows of Poetry.*" Unpublished Manuscript 49-50

PLACES

We decided to visit Kenya because my sister Joan was working there. She was a licensed midwife, but her motivation was as a Christian missionary. Among the close community of Christian families in Kenya she met the Brysons: Edgar, Nancy, and their three daughters. Nancy, sadly, was drowned in a ferry boat accident traveling between Northern Ireland and Scotland. In 1955 Edgar married Joan, thus presenting Joan with three step-daughters and me with three step-nieces: Margaret, Jennifer and Rosaleen.

Our introduction to Kenya was preceded by a visit to Vienna, where Eugene's oldest brother Marcel was living with his second wife Ilonka, originally from Hungary. The contrast between the two visits could not have been more vivid. It was January, and we found Vienna bone-chillingly cold. It was not that the temperature was any lower than Colorado's but the factor of damp in the climate made all the difference.

A memory of a brief visit to then-Communist Hungary with Marcel and Ilonka stays in my mind. We were in a little store filled with delicious pastries. After asking us which we would like to sample, Marcel signaled to an employee standing behind the counter, with her back against the wall. "We would like some of these, and these, and these," he requested, in Hungarian. She said something to him, but did not move. He made an astonished comment, then turned to us and said, "Can you believe it, she says she is not here yet!" So much for the Communist version of customer service.

Landing in Nairobi was wonderfully warm. We had a once-in-a-lifetime holiday in Kenya. The majority of our time was spent as guests of Charles and Margaret Njonjo. We enjoyed getting to know something of Charles' background and interests. He was a member of the Kikuyu tribe, largest of the many tribes in Kenya, who had received his legal education in South Africa and Britain. His father was a tribal chief. He rose to political prominence in the years before

Kenya achieved its hard-won independence, and was appointed Attorney General by Jomo Kenyatta, the country's first President.

Margaret was an incredible hostess who arranged a busy and fascinating schedule for us. This included an overnight stay in the Aberdares, one of the prime wildlife viewing areas, a flight around Mt. Kenya in a small plane, and a memorable visit to a large farm outside Rongai. This was the home of Edgar's middle daughter, Jennifer. Her husband Fred was the manager of this productive estate. The most vivid memory that I have of that brief experience is a nighttime one. Soon after we had said goodnight and walked to our attractive little guest house, Fred turned off a switch – and all the lights in our house, in the main house and in the scattered homes of the farm workers went out. The intense darkness was almost palpable – and the sky was studded with stars more huge and brilliant than any I have ever seen, before or since.[3]

[3] Sternberg, Barbara. "*Through Windows of Poetry.*" Unpublished Manuscript 85-86

Kate Van Wyhe

MY HISTORICAL LANDMARKS

Mom believes the godless Japanese will conquer us and march on Kansas City. She writes notes to that affect in my baby scrapbook.

I see Movietone News of withered bones piled high in concentration camps and the aftermath of the atomic bomb when all I want to see is Doris Day singing in a pretty-clothes picture.

I am conductor of the kindergarten rhythm band, resplendent in plumed hat and satin costume. I can't get the triangle dinger to come in on cue, so I fret whether our final performance will be a success.

In first grade, Tim Conway holds my sweaty hand and kisses it during a Jesus movie. Does this mean we are both now passengers on the express train to hell?

Pudgy Sister Ursula tells us in third grade that Communists will knock on the classroom door and ask if we believe in Christ. We are all to say we do, of course, and then they will chop off our heads. Let the chopping begin! Sister Ursula is old and can't wait for martyrdom. I am still young and am just getting used to my head where it is.

By 1947, Mother has switched worrying and praying to stop Russia, the Red Menace, from conquering us and marching on Kansas City.

On a happier note, while Sister Yvonne's back is turned in the cafeteria, I make Francie Scholz laugh and spew milk out her nose.

Mother becomes more optimistic and once more switches her praying for God to protect the new leader and great Catholic freedom fighter, Fidel Castro, who will save his people and make the world a safer place for all of us.

The country is seized with the Cuban missile crisis. We are told there are bombs offshore waiting to snuff our whole country. The more enterprising and athletic are building bomb shelters and stockpiling Campbell's soup, and pork and beans. My family eats Rice Krispie treats, watches TV, and waits to be annihilated.

Kennedy and our innocence are dead. Vietnam creeps slowly into our consciousness. Although Mother worries about the godless Vietnamese, she feels they are too poor and disorganized to reach Kansas City undetected.

Charlotte von Bayern

CHRISTMAS AT MY GRANDFATHER'S HOUSE

It is December in the northern Bavarian hills. The land is blanketed in deep snow. Winter is here to stay. Christmas is not far off. "Your grandfather does not celebrate Christmas," I was told before I came to live with him. "He does not know what Christmas is," they said. I can't imagine life without Christmas.

As far back as I can remember Christmas has been the most magical time of the year. Listening to the rustling and tinkling behind closed doors, imagining the Christkindl performing his magic on Christmas Eve. And then at the end of the day the doors open to a wonder. There is the tree from floor to ceiling, ablaze in a thousand candles and sparklers, my father at the piano playing those lyrical songs that are only sung on Christmas Eve. The floor is laden with presents, the table decked with confections that have been wafting their aroma through the entire house for weeks. One has to have lived that anticipation and imagined the activity that accompanied the mysterious tingling sounds and the hushed rustling that went on all day in order to understand the thrill when those doors are opened. Even at eight and nine years old I could not believe that my father, who was behind those closed doors all day, could be entirely responsible for all this magic. There must be a Christkindl to help him.

So now Christmas is nearing. I've been in this strange place with my grandfather for six months and I don't know how to go about telling him about Christmas. "Your grandfather doesn't know what Christmas is," they had said. How could someone not know about Christmas? Surely if there is a Christkindl he must have come to this part of the land too. Maybe my grandfather kept his doors and windows locked. Maybe if I tell him that the windows and shutters must stay unlocked. But then, maybe it's all really not true. Maybe...but it must be. I have to find a way to convince him!

Only five days now. My grandfather says tomorrow we will go to the high forest and find a tree. I'm not sure he really understands about Christmas trees. But the anticipation almost bursts my heart. Never have I been part of finding a Christmas tree in the very forest!

I can hear the old alarm clock's shrill scream even across the wide hall in my grandfather's house. But I am already awake. "Must get up early," my grandfather had said, "in order to get to the forest and back." Today I don't need reminders. We are going to get a Christmas tree! But how does one find a Christmas tree? I run to the big kitchen; the enormous black woodstove is still warm. Like every morning, I lay my cold clothes on the warming shelf and dress by the side of the stove where the cat is snuggled. I wonder *Is it possible that we might run into the Christkindl?* I want so much for my grandfather to know about the real Christmas.

Off we trek. We have to hike out of the valley, up to the plateau, and cross the high tundra to get to the forest where the Tannenbaum grow. The stars are still out when we start our climb. By the time we get to the edge of the high tundra the sun streams across the vast expanse and fills it with a fiery glow. The white snow looks as if it is on fire. I have never been here before. I have seen pictures of the ocean. This looks like a flaming ocean. And there across the vast expanse is the Tannenbaum forest. I recognize it by its tall spires and the perfect shape of the trees.

The tundra is windswept. My grandfather takes my hand so I can keep up with him. At times I have to walk behind him and step in his footsteps because I sink to my hips in snow drifts. The stillness makes the crunch of our steps echo across the plain. Grandfather explains that this is sheep grazing land. Thousands of sheep live here all summer until they get herded down the valley to winter in giant pens. I imagine the sheepdogs gathering the sheep from this endless field. And I see myself as the shepherd leading the way to the valley.

The forest grows taller and the trees become greener. I see a tree a hundred meters away and I know it's the perfect tree, but as we get closer I can see it is as tall as a church steeple. Grandfather keeps examining trees and rejecting trees. He says we must find a tree that is full and round. Finally he cuts down a tree with his hatchet. I think it is much too small. It looks like a baby tree. I watch as grandfather ties a thick rope around the tree so we can drag it across the tundra. We walk in our original footsteps. When we reach the edge of the plateau he has to carry the tree down to the valley. Suddenly it looks monstrous. His face and shoulders are buried inside the tree. I am cold to the bone and at the same time glowing inside. Our very own Christmas tree, found in the forest.

It has to "fall out" grandfather says as he fastens the tree in a massive crossbar stand and tucks it in a sheltered space between the house and the woodshed. Tomorrow is Sunday. Grandfather says we need to make decorations for our tree. I still remember my mother baking Christmas tree cookies when I was very small. But I have never heard of making ornaments. Ornaments are made by glass blowers and woodcarvers and maybe angels.

As I awake in the morning I can already smell the fragrance of cinnamon and cloves and anise. There on the stone sill in the kitchen is a giant ball of dough curing; "to make it leathery," my grandfather explains. I keep poking to see how leathery it is but it will have to cure for hours.

Meanwhile there are other things to prepare. On the table is a bowl full of walnuts and an old candy box filled with gold and silver wrappers, wrinkled and tattered. It looks like they are wrappers from fancy chocolates and cigarettes and such. He must have save those for years. My task is to press the foil against the walnut shells and make it look like gilded skin. He bores holes and fastens sticks and wires for hangers. Another basket is filled with pinecones which I had thought are for burning. I am allowed to paint the tips white for snow and he makes hangers for those as well. Next he shows me a long branch that has fifteen strings suspended from it. I dip the strings into a tin can of melted wax; each string requires thirty dips. These will be the candles for the tree. While I make the candles my grandfather sits in his large leather chair and makes strange wire spirals. I have to guess what they are. Are they to hang the nuts from or are they wire bells? No, they will be holders for the candles.

"Candles must be wired onto the tree branches, otherwise they will tilt," Grandfather explains. When my candles are as thick as my thumb and twice as long, he takes the branch with the hanging candles and moves it outside the deep window frame; "to let them harden," he says.

Now the dough is ready to be worked. The big table gets cleared off and we start rolling out big slabs of this glistening brown mass. My grandfather takes one of his small carving knives and start cutting away. This is truly magic. What appears are birds and pigs and angels and stars of all shapes and sizes and even a chimney sweep. I get to lift them off the table and onto flat tin sheets. My grandfather takes a wooden match and bores holes in the cookies to lace a string for hanging them on the tree. When he is done cutting there are a lot of scraps that we place on another tin sheet to bake and have with hot milk. The aroma of the baking lebkuchen is more than a ten-year-old heart can contain. I hug this old man who had never come closer to me than holding my hand. One time he lifted me so I could reach the ceiling to pin a mobile of paper birds in front of the large garden window. Today I hug him.

Christmas Eve the tree which has by then fallen out for four days is brought inside the house. This baby tree, as I thought it was, towers to the very ceiling of the parlor and looks majestic in front of the garden window. Grandfather trims the lower branches and fills in some bare spots on the tree. "A Christmas tree must be round and perfect," he says, "no big gaps."

Now we dress this fine hand-picked forest tree with all the finery that we prepared the past few days. First comes the angel on the very top. It is made largely from sheep's wool which has been washed in lye soap and combed to a fine luster. It looks like spun gold. Apples are hung on the strong inside branches. Then we work down from the top. We distribute the golden and silver nuts and the cookies throughout the tree. My grandfather wires the candles toward the outer branches. "We can only hang lightweight ornaments on the tiny outer twigs." So I get to hang the pinecones on the tips. They glow in the dusk.

There it stands in all its splendor, glistening and sparkling, each item in a perfect spot. This is the most special Christmas tree ever.

Tonight we go to Midnight Mass. We get dressed in our Sunday outfits, I in my new woolen jacket with the stitched-on oak leaves and real silver buttons. But before we go, we light all the candles with the willow stick as long as my arm. We stand in awe. Then my grandfather pulls a reed flute out of a flannel bag and plays a haunting tune. If there ever were a Christkindl I know how he must feel on Christmas Eve, for tonight my grandfather and I recaptured the mystery of that magic night.

THE FINAL WEEKS OF WORLD WAR II IN A REMOTE VALLEY IN BAVARIA

It is spring 1945. The war has been going on for five and a half years. The past year has been debilitating. Everyone is exhausted, all resources depleted, cars and buses appropriated to the war effort long ago, the shops empty, no goods even if you have points left on your ration cards. It's been six months since the last crops were harvested, hardly any new crops planted, no vegetables, no potatoes; the radishes get pulled before they are mature. We are waiting for the end of the war, the end of this madness.

Dresden, seemingly of no military value, heretofore had been spared, now was carpet-bombed, more than 100,000 casualties (mostly women and children). Two weeks later Pforzheim carpet-bombed, not a house left standing; two weeks after that Wurzburg. Will our beloved Munich be next? Here too no military or industrial value in destroying it, but that no longer seems to matter.

The last few weeks planes have been strafing our small village in an attempt to destroy the bridges that connect the only railroad line between Munich and Salzburg. The bombs are not successful in destroying the bridges but are very successful in terrorizing the locals: windows shattered, roofs caved in, women and children strafed as they run for shelter. Frau Prechtl is determined to pick wild lettuce as she does every April; when the squadron of planes approaches she runs for shelter under one of the bridges. Her father chides her, "Don't you know they are after the bridges?" But she won't be deterred from her annual mission.

Farmer Lang, with the help of some POWs, has built a tunnel shelter into the mountain for the women and children. There is not much lighting in the tunnel so the women are knitting and mending outside. Very quickly the children lose interest in playing in the tunnel so they fight and cry. The Leitmeir sisters, who both lost their husbands, tell stories about the last war. When the alarm bell rings to alert an impending attack, the women scramble for what they think is the safest spot inside the tunnel. Everyone goes home at night and tomorrow they repeat the ritual.

The Allied forces are advancing daily. The combat zone is now on German soil; our own cities and towns looted and burned; our own people humiliated and terrorized. We are all glued to the radios: Where are the French today? How far have the English advanced? Who will arrive in southern Bavaria first? Will it be the Russians or the Americans? Who is more likely to spare the women and children? Will they round up and kill all the old men and young boys? Rumors have been swarming for months. What to believe? Radio broadcasts are infrequent and contain sketchy information.

Then we hear from neighboring villages the German army is retreating. The war has come to our backyard. We don't know what war in your backyard looks like. Will they find us in our dirt bunker in the mountain? Today the first German troops arrived from the west. They don't look like an army. Their uniforms are tattered and dirty. They look like they have not shaved or washed in months. Most are on foot, their boots shredded. At night they pitch tents and bed down. It is raining, the tents in a mud field. Tomorrow they move on, leaving behind an abandoned tank next to a barn. After several waves of German retreats, the last being the Waffen SS, there are two days of silence. And endless rain.

We are waiting for the German retreat from the Eastern Front. The tension mounts. The Russians have taken Salzburg in the east; the Americans have taken Munich in the west. Who will take us? The young women have all cut their hair, dress like young boys, and hide in the bunker. We have heard of the atrocities when the Russians invaded East Prussia. Grandmother Lang says the British are more civilized conquerors. We have by now given up hope it will be the English; they are too far north. The common notion is that the Americans may not be as bad as the Russians.

Now there is silence. For two more days. Who will come next? There is no retreating German army coming from the Eastern Front.

It is a splendid sunny April morning. We hear the rumbling of vehicles in the distant west. Some brave individuals climb the railroad tracks to reconnoiter. "It's an army!" Must be the Americans. We hang white sheets from our windows and balconies. Someone advises us to stand in front of our houses, "Don't hide inside; that arouses suspicion." The advancing army moves slowly along our narrow country road. First the tanks, twenty-seven of them, with a white star emblazoned on their front. Then the trucks, canvas covered; we don't know if they are filled with soldiers or ammunition. We don't know if they will jump out and ambush us. Clusters of scared people stand and stare. Tante Wilhelmina is wearing her Bavarian costume which she usually only wears to weddings and festivals. Now come the jeeps, roofless, some with American flags, their occupants stare straight ahead. It is all so surreal like a three-dimensional frieze in an Egyptian tomb moving along on a conveyor belt. There are no foot soldiers.

If the soldiers in jeeps stole a glance sideways they would see motley clusters of seemingly deaf and dumb peasants. Farmer Lang is holding his German Shepherd on a leash. The Leitmeir sisters are jointly hugging their Dachshund. Children in their thrice-handed-down clothes look like waifs in a melodrama. I turned fourteen two weeks ago. I can speak English. I want to shout, "We are harmless!" but I am too frightened; so I, like the others, stand and watch the convoy move along.

The German army retreats another week and the American army follows until they reach the Bohemian Forest. The Americans leave behind a small command to secure order in our valley. We are now in limbo, still at war, under siege and house arrest by the enemy, waiting for the end.

The end of World War II will be declared in seven days. It is mostly anticlimactic.

How do we begin to rebuild our lives?

THE PENNSYLVANIA TURNPIKE

We are now getting on the famous Pennsylvania Turnpike. It is a toll road. That means you have to pay to drive on it. But it is indeed a beautiful road: double lanes in both directions and a grassy median strip to divide them. Just like the Autobahn. So we will be able to virtually fly to Pittsburgh.

But, oh my, when the speed reaches fifty or sixty miles per hour the car goes thumpety-thumpety-thump. "What is that?" I ask. "It's the concrete slabs," Harold says, "You'll get used to it." Hmmm .... We thumpety-thumpety-thump along.

The brochure says that we will cross the Allegheny Mountains via seven tunnels. The countryside is breathtakingly beautiful, mostly forests and some farmland. No towns, no people, no animals. A mountain range in the far distance, also covered in forest.

A Howard Johnson's Ice Cream Shop, 28 flavors of ice cream. We whiz by. We can't stop, we must get to Pittsburgh before dark. I can't even imagine what these twenty-eight flavors could be.

Harold is listening to the radio ... *Comeonamyhouse my house-y comeon...I'll give you everything...*

I'm thinking how exciting it was back home when we could get chocolate ice cream in addition to vanilla, how we would run to each house and proclaim, "They are having chocolate today!" That was so exciting.

We reach the first tunnel; it is incredible, just like the railroad tunnels in Switzerland. So long and smooth, we are going through the mountain at a slow pace. I have my conversion sheet at hand: 4541 feet is 1.38 kilometers. When we come out the other side more forest. More thumpety-thump.

In Germany we have the Autobahn; you glide on it as on air. There are not very many cars in Germany, but the roads don't go thumpety-thump.

We rumble on at a fast pace. No towns. New song: *Jambalayoo... we'll have big fun in the bayoo, sonofagun... in the bayou...*

I'm remembering the first time I tasted ice cream; it was at the Munich railroad station, a street vendor with a small cart. It was so special.

And, here, another Howard Johnson's Ice Cream Shop. Twenty-eight flavors! We can't stop, we must get to Pittsburgh before dark.

I try to imagine what all the twenty-eight flavors might be. Can't think beyond vanilla and chocolate. Harold says there is also a mint flavor. And what are the other twenty-five flavors?

We are approaching another tunnel. It's unbelievable that we are going under the mountain and coming out on the other side. This one is even longer than the first, 6,070 feet, more than two kilometers.

Along the turnpike it is harder to study the car models; we can only see the backs of the cars.

I wish I could find out the twenty-eight flavors of ice cream. What could all these flavors be?

Another song: *How much is that doggie in the window... With a waggle-y tail ... I want that doggie in the window ...*

All told, five mountains, seven tunnels, a dozen songs I don't understand, and eleven Ice Cream Shops. But we must get to Pittsburgh before dark.

After three hours, a sign: *Pennsylvania Turnpike ... End 2 miles.* And another sign: *Toll Gate, Exit at Irwin, Prepare to Stop.* We will find an Ice Cream Shop in Pittsburgh.

Finally, no more thumpety-thump. We eat dinner at Dan's Grille. Chicken fried steak, which looks somewhat like Wienerschnitzel. Tastes great, but mashed potatoes instead of potato salad. The lemon meringue pie tastes wonderful.

There is no Howard Johnson's Ice Cream Shop in Pittsburgh. I still wonder what the other twenty-five flavors could be.

Tomorrow I will buy some new American summer clothes. And then we will go through Ohio.

Si Weir

AN OPEN DOOR POLICY

September 1973 marked the end of a long hot summer on Chicago's South Side. It also marked the continuing protests of a radical group of University of Chicago students, black activists, and young adults who would become the Chicago Weather Underground and in part the Chicago Seven. It was this group of seven who would stand accused in a famous trial for anarchistic activities.

This group, then called the Committee Against Racist Medical Care (CARMEC), was protesting the alleged deaths of two community black males due to denial of care or poor care at the University of Chicago Hospital (UCH) and a nearby community hospital. A march was to take place at the UCH on Saturday, September 26, 1973 at noon. Unfortunately, I was the on-call administrator at UCH and would plan our resistance to the anticipated attempt to enter the main hospital lobby, trash offices, set fires, and attempt to shut down the emergency department.

It is incorrect to say I would plan our defenses. In fact, the University Security would plan defenses at the direction of the University administration. The University was very cautious when dealing with protests that involved students. It followed the theme of "Let's reason together," believing that negotiations led to acceptable solutions. On the other hand, the Chicago Police Department believed protests should be broken with physical force if necessary, and that intimidation paid the highest dividends in solving confrontations. In short, the Chicago police busted heads first and negotiated later.

On Saturday September 26 at 10 a.m. as defense plans were being put in place and protesters were gathering, my boss, the Director of the University of Chicago Hospitals, called from home and offered his own plan. "Don't let the bastards through our front doors. If you need to, call in the Chicago police Gang Squad and tell University Security to get the hell out of the way." Shortly thereafter, the University's security chief arrived with six campus officers and our hospital day shift officers, Paddy Finnegan and Roosevelt Brown, a short, very muscular black man. The chief offered that he was present to give me "All the support you'll need today."

At about 11:30 a.m., the CPD watch commander for our police district arrived and, glowering at the University security chief said, "We have two plain clothes officers in the march as well as an armed police photographer to take pictures and harass the leaders. One of the leaders may react and we'll step in and arrest them. In case things get out of control, I have forty-five riot-trained officers on a bus at 52nd and Cottage Grove." Finally, to soothe my growing sense that things were already out of control, the commander said, "Young man, you're our point person. If you can't protect the front door, we move in and throw a lot of bad people in Cook County Jail." Somehow, I had become a point man, the man of the hour. The police commander wanted to maintain the fiction that I, not forty-five helmeted cops on a bus, was in control. This fiction would appease the University security chief and the administration.

And so the marchers arrived on the long double sidewalk leading from the street back to the hospital main entrance. The main entrance was two oak doors, heavy with brass fittings, handles, pull bars and chrome steel panic bars, with carved figures of famous physicians and pleading patients. There we stood, Paddy Finnegan, a beyond-his-prime ex-prize fighter and Roosevelt Brown, pugnacious and strong enough for most heavy work, and I, a newly minted and untested hospital administrator. "Nobody gets in," I ordered, and Paddy and Roosevelt sprang to the right door, as the chanting began.

"Tear it down! Tear it down!"

"End racism now!"

"End it here!"

Several young roughly-dressed males and two young women in tank tops and jeans leaped to the right door and pulled it a little open. "Pull the door, Roosevelt!!" I said, trying to quell a shaky voice. "Yes, here it comes. Paddy, grab the panic bar!" Screaming and hoarse yelling ensued as Roosevelt smoothly pulled the door shut, his arms acting like hydraulic rams. "Nice work," I said as Finnegan straightened his hat, which during the assault on the door had turned backward on his head. The crowd stood outside pounding on the door, shouting, "Racists, murderers, murderers!"

Finnegan, Roosevelt, the crowd, and I, had assumed the great left door was locked tight. Just then, Carl Nighswonger, the hospital chaplain, opened the left door and entered the lobby! "Good morning," he greeted us kindly, "What's that crowd about?" As one, the crowd howling, leaped to the left door! And Roosevelt, quick as a cat, leaped past Paddy and me, pulled the door shut and locked it. We were saved! Just then the police bus stopped on the street in front of the main entrance. Several large and heavily armored police got out and marched to the doors. The protest ended with shouts and murmurs.

As I look back almost a half century, I wonder about the CPD and University Security fighting more over contested territory than protecting the hospital and its patients and staff. I wonder if the protesters are as certain and angry about issues today as they were in the 70s. I recall that the CPD today still breaks heads first, and worse. Mostly, I wonder about Carl Nighswonger, the affable chaplain, walking through the angry screaming crowd. "Tear it down, tear it down."

"Yes, yes," Carl might have said, smiling at snarls and stares, patting backs as they struggled at the left door. Then he entered the right door, as he had for years. *Perhaps a group of tourists,* he might have thought, as he crossed the lobby, walking past the emergency department entrance and to the elevator, which would deliver him to the patient floors, where he would pastor to the ill and champion the poor and marginalized.

A NEW ADVENTURE IN A DESERT HOSPITAL

We left Abha Airport, which was perched on the edge of the escarpment leading down to the Red Sea and located in the far southwest of Saudi Arabia. We drove east then south following Toyota pickup trucks carrying live animals, mainly goats. We drove past the Saudi airbase to the Saudi Military City. It was a hot dusty mid-afternoon and most of the gate guards were fast asleep in their room next to the main gate. We were allowed entry by a sleepy twenty-year-old in a uniform meant for a larger man. He carried a US Thompson submachine gun, right out of a 1930's Chicago gangland movie. Like the Tommy gun the actors carried, the sleepy soldier's gun carried no bullets. Close by, we arrived at the King Faisal Military Hospital, where I was to be the new hospital director, the new Modeir Mustafa.

In Saudi Arabia trees were a luxury and only find a home in important places. The hospital, one story and in the form of a square with an open center courtyard, was surrounded by trees. The hospital courtyard was dominated by an open-air mosque, aligned perfectly to the degree with the compass heading toward Mecca. The north and south sides contained open wards for males and females, each with about fifty beds. The west side of the hospital contained the special care units: a neonatal ICU, an adult ICU, a pediatrics unit, and a burn unit. In all, the hospital was about the size of a smaller American community hospital, but the bed allocation matched the needs of army families. The large newborn ICU was needed for Saudi babies, who often received little prenatal care. The burn unit, unheard of in a US community hospital, was for a community who cooked over open fires or charcoal or over gas grills. The pediatrics unit was for Saudi children here in the desert, who were chronically dehydrated. One episode of vomiting or diarrhea could be fatal if not treated within two hours.

And so I entered a land of discovery, a hospital of discovery. A land of Third World living, of Bedouins cooking over open fires, of patients dying from snake bites untreated. All of this in a setting of the world's greatest military technology, tanks and Bradley Fighting Vehicles. And overhead, the sky howled with fighter jets coming and going from the Saudi airbase. Most of this equipment was sold by the US government to a desert people who had driven automobiles for only one generation. Alcohol was forbidden in the kingdom, but grape juice bottled by a Royal Family company, and offered for sale in local grocery stores, met the exact requirements for wine making: the right sugar content, pH, and rubber-stoppered bottles. At the end of our first day "in Kingdom", evening prayer was called out by loudspeaker from the village mosque. First a clearing of the throat of the local muezzin, and then singing in Arabic, "There is only one God and Mohamed is his messenger." Then all responded, in the mosque and all around the military city, in Arabic but the same as in English, "Amen."

PROHIBITION SAUDI STYLE

There we stood in the high Saudi desert, at 2:30 a.m., under the star-blazed sky. Our small group of King Faisal Hospital staff was hard at work, breaking bottles of wine. Bob, our Human Resources Manager, called out the totals. "Fifty bottles of aged Chardonnay. Very high quality." He licked his lips after a sip from an open bottle. "Twenty seven bottles of young and probably low quality Merlot." Reds were always difficult to obtain in Saudi Arabia. They took months to age to a point where they could be enjoyed. On the contrary, white wines could be aged in secret closets or in the maid quarters of married housing. Whites aged quickly and could be served after only weeks of aging. I once asked a friend the age of the cloudy white wine we were sipping. He looked at his watch!

Then we turned to the beer. Bob and Larry, an assistant at the hospital, tipped over ten five-gallon pails of fermenting beer. We followed this by breaking twenty-two bottles of what appeared to be nice English bitter, made by an auto mechanic in our transportation department who was from York in England. Finally, we focused on the hard alcohol. Being a new hospital director in Saudi, I was stunned by the amount and variety of hard liquor, here in a country that forbade any alcoholic beverage and that deported expatriates who fermented or imbibed alcohol. In fact, the reason we stood alone in the desert at two a.m. breaking bottles was that Saudi military police, who had raided the hospital staff living quarters searching for alcohol, were terrified to be involved in any way with counting or destroying alcohol, lest Saudi military intelligence claim the police had diverted booze for their own use.

Twelve bottles of Sidici, like American white lightning, and meaning *My Friend*, were emptied in the sand. Then we counted and destroyed four bottles of the Saudi version of Grand Marnier, which was made by hanging an orange over a wide-mouth bottle of Sidici and covering it all with cotton 4x4s. Alcohol vapors and the rotting orange would allow orange oil to drip into the alcohol. After several weeks a passable, if crude, Grand Marnier would appear. By 3:45

a.m. our work was completed, bottles and pails and small stills were loaded in a small truck for burial further in the desert. But Aunni Abu Sabha, another staff member and our main translator, said, "Aren't there only four of us?" I noted that there should indeed be four: Aunni, Bob, Larry, and I. "Well then," Aunni said, "Who is this guy?" Stunned, I turned in the darkness to find a Bedouin, in full desert dress standing with the group. Aunni asked the man in Arabic why he was here. The man said he had heard bottles breaking and smelled alcohol from his house about a half mile away. This was certainly true. All non-drinking Saudis have an intense sensitivity to the smell of alcohol. "What are you doing?" the Bedouin asked.

Aunni answered, "We're on secret government work with the support of Sheik of Abha. This is confidential work. Please leave and keep our secret." The Bedouin bade us farewell and with a bow, while patting his chest, disappeared into the desert darkness. His encounter with a bunch of Westerners probably drinking alcohol would be spread to his friends; then to the Sheik of Abha; and then to General Kalifha via the Sheik by noon the next day. The General, head of the Medical Services Division of the Ministry of Defense and Aviation, the Saudi Armed Forces, would send a note to me via the Project Director, my new boss, asking for a full investigation of the *desert story and alcohol.* The Project Director already knew the "Desert Story," having arranged a quick Kingdom exit for three physicians and three staff members found with booze in their houses, who were certain to be expelled very soon.

At the time, I wondered about my experiences in Saudi Arabia. Breaking wine bottles? Secret government work? Hospital staff deported? What was I doing there? I was an experienced and well-trained hospital director, come to save Saudi Armed Forces and their families through the introduction of modern high-quality health care. How the hell had I come to this? Shoes soaked in beer and bad wine? Hands sticky from rotten oranges? Chilled — like beer kept cold for the daytime desert heat?

Now almost a half century later after a full career as a hospital administrator, I can look back at my time in Saudi Arabia as a time of testing and professional growth, as a time of developing a toughness under stress and an ability to think on my feet in any situation, even in the dark, even in the high desert.

Louise M. Whiteside

A TRIP DOWNTOWN

The green and white bus squealed to a stop directly in front of the bus stop at Fifth and Ingraham Streets. Hopping up the two steps to the conductor's box, I dropped my dime into the narrow slot and cautiously balanced my way to a seat midway between front and back, being sure to sit next to a window.

Those special Saturday afternoons in 1951 Washington, D.C. – when Mom would hand me a dollar bill – plus two dimes for round-trip bus fare – were infrequent and glorious. At twelve, I was thrilled to have a whole afternoon – and an entire dollar – to do whatever the time and money would allow.

Sitting in the green leather seat, I drank in the endless stream of row houses, some with large porches and turreted roofs; leaned sideways as the bus wound around Grant Circle, where the old stone, steepled, Gothic-style St. Gabriel's Catholic Church stood. St. Gabriel's mystified me: my Catholic friends had talked to me about going to confession, and I'd watched the girls return from school in their navy-blue wool dresses with little white collars, but I couldn't fathom what went on behind those heavy, arched wooden church doors.

The bus rounded Logan Circle. Downtown wasn't far away now. Soon I'd head for Murphy's Five and Ten – Murphy's, at Thirteenth and F Streets – where I'd amble through aisles of candy and cosmetics and dishes and pretty lacy underthings – for as long as I could make my dollar last.

Thirteenth and F Streets. I pulled the cord above the window to signal the driver to stop. But he'd have stopped anyway: this was the middle of the downtown shopping district, and a crowd of people was getting off with me.

I virtually floated down the bus steps and onto the busy sidewalk, making my way the half block to Murphy's.

As I stepped inside the heavy, swinging doors, the mixed aroma of caramel candy, salted nuts, and perfumed soap filled my nostrils. I could hear a woman's voice on a loud speaker, urging customers to come downstairs and buy rugs and shower curtains at a bargain price. Men and women hovered in front of rows of counters, contemplating combs and billfolds and stockings.

But the downstairs lunch counter was pulling me: it was past lunchtime, and a tuna fish sandwich on white toast, with a small Coke in an old-fashioned fountain glass, awaited me.

A delicious forty cents now spent on lunch, I knew I had to budget my additional sixty cents very frugally.

A shimmery pink lipstick was next; then, a package of note paper with a picture of a little angel on the front of each page, along with the caption, "How are you, for Heaven's sake?" Finally, a tiny sack of swirly caramel creams claimed the remainder of my dollar.

With two and a half hours and one dollar bill spent, my feet now moving a little more slowly, I climbed on board the J-6 bus marked "Takoma," slumped into a window seat once more, and promptly nodded off until the bus reached the corner of Fifth and Ingraham Streets – one block from my house.

I think about those downtown excursions – of the excitement, the freedom, and the grown-upness of going all the way downtown alone. I think of the overwhelming, almost circus-like feeling of Murphy's Five and Ten. I think of the joy of purchasing items of my own liking. But mostly I marvel at what a dollar used to buy!

A VISIT TO CHURCH

I remember visiting St. Gabriel's Roman Catholic Church with girlfriends Tilly and Trilby in the summer of 1949. I'd seen the old stone, Gothic-style church at Grant Circle many times, but had never had the chance for an *inside* look until now. St. Gabriel's reminded me somewhat of a medieval castle: its great steeples and turrets towering over the little concrete-and-brick northwest Washington, D.C. neighborhood where I lived.

Tilly pulled hard on the huge brass door handle, and one of the massive wooden double doors opened to us. It was a Wednesday afternoon; no other churchgoers were in sight. I followed the girls into a musty-smelling, stone-hewn lobby: floors, walls, ceilings of cold gray rock surrounded us. I watched as each girl dipped a forefinger and middle finger into a small, golden, water-filled bowl hanging just inside the entryway – and then touched those fingers to her forehead, her breastbone, and to one shoulder at a time.

My friends now led me through a set of inner, translucent, cut-glass doors, engraved with crosses. The wet, almost mildew smell of the church – reminiscent of my own family basement after a week of soaking rain – filled my nostrils. Sunlight poured through magnificent, arched, red, gold and blue glass windows which displayed biblical characters. My own breath sounded to me loud and intrusive in the silence. Candles in tiny red glasses flickered across the front of the sanctuary, and statues of flowing-robed, plaster saints stared from the sidelines. On the left-front wall of the sanctuary hung an eight-or-ten-foot-high wooden cross with a life-sized (and amazingly lifelike) figure of a blood-stained Jesus nailed to it. I could feel little bumps raising up on my forearms.

I looked on as Tilly – then Trilby – touched one knee to the cold, stony aisle floor, entered a pew, and knelt once again – only this time with both knees – onto a long, narrow, brown-padded board about three inches from the floor. Repeating the forehead, breastbone and shoulder ritual, each closed her eyes, bowed her head low, and moved her lips silently for three – five – maybe ten minutes. Then, rising, moving out of the pew space, and repeating the one-knee-to-floor exercise a final time, the girls exited the sanctuary with me — wide-eyed and silent — in tow.

I felt no emotion and asked no questions during our half-hour walk through familiar Washington streets. But the memory of what I'd just experienced would be inside me for life.

Today the flickering, red candles; the musty, stony smell of the sanctuary; the gorgeous arched, sunlit, stained-glass windows; the sculptured saints; and the almost-lifelike figure of a wounded Jesus dead upon the cross stay — brilliant and burning — in my senses.

What was this little, 10-year-old, Jewish, D.C. girl feeling while inside St. Gabriel's Church? Looking back, I can almost compare the experience to gazing at a mist-covered mountain peak or at an orangey-pink desert sunset. Was it awe? Or wonder? Or love?

I recall the feelings, but no words come to mind.

Contributors

LYNN ALLBRIGHT was born in Nashville, Tennessee. She moved to Albuquerque, Santa Barbara, Colorado Springs, Guadalajara, and settled in Morrison, Colorado with her unique and wonderful family. Her education includes a Bachelor's Degree in Painting and Psychology with a K-1 teaching certification, a Master's Degree in Painting and Drawing, and Doctoral work in Critical Studies. The written word in all of these scenarios has forever been a fascination, a notepad is always with her. "Carolyn Campbell's writing classes have helped give sense and structure to these words for over eight years. Learning to speak and read these words has been a gift beyond my dreams!"

PAULA BARD is a writer and artist. She works with writing, photography, intaglio printmaking and textiles. Her artwork is exhibited both locally and nationally. In addition to the life-long art making, she has worked as an art magazine editor, marketing director, writer, and she has taught art. She lives with her family and maintains a studio on a mountaintop in Morrison, CO. Education: B.F.A and B.A. in English, in 1980, Colorado State University, Fort Collins, CO.

JEAN BARRINGER was born in London in 1926 and grew up during the blitz of London during WWII, spending most nights in a bomb shelter. At age eighteen she joined the British Women's Army and spent three years as an Army driver. She married Anthony Barringer in 1948 and after he graduated with a Ph.D. from the Royal School of Mines, emigrated to Canada in March of 1954 with her four-month-old baby one month after her husband. They lived in Toronto for six months then transferred to New Brunswick for one year and then for six months in Ottawa. She and Anthony had four more children, all born in Canada. The family immigrated to Colorado in 1977 where she now lives.

JEAN BELL is a retired computer science professor, a potter and a poet. She is the author of two books: *Love, Teeta,* a biography based on letters her mother wrote during the 1940's; and *At Home on Blue Creek,* poems reflecting the sights and sounds around her home in the beautiful Rocky Mountains. In addition to writing, Jean enjoys teaching compassionate communication, hiking, babysitting her grandchildren, travel and other adventures with her husband, family, and friends.

KATHI BERNIER was born in 1941 in Glendale, CA. She graduated Phi Beta Kappa and Magna Cum Laude from USC with a degree in educational development. She and her first husband Larry joined the Peace Corps and were stationed in Sri Lanka. Their son Dan was born during their Peace Corps tour. Upon returning to California, she completed a Doctoral Degree in Education from UCLA. After her divorce she and her son Dan lived in Germany for several years then they returned to Fairfax, VA where she wrote, traveled and taught special education for ten years and where she met and married Jim Bernier. Jim and Kathi moved to Colorado in 1992 and traveled extensively to Europe, Greece, Asia, China and Russia. Kathi writes poetry and enjoys telling stories of her many adventures.

CONNIE BIERKAN was born and adopted in 1952, raised as an only child and lived in America until 1961. Her formative years were spent in Zürich and London where she travelled throughout Europe, became fluent in French and German, and validated her freshman year of college thanks to such a rigorous British education. She graduated Skidmore College in 1974 with a B.A. in English Literature and a minor in Semantics. Along with marriage, two daughters, divorce and a second marriage to best friend, Kurt, she has volunteered with the elderly, the sick and for political endeavors both on the state and national level. She is an expert stitcher of needlepoint and budding writer of memoir and prose poetry. Classes with Carolyn Campbell are the highlight of her week.

CAROLYN EVANS CAMPBELL is a writer, poet, teacher and artist in the Evergreen region. Her six books of poetry, a historical novel, a memoir and a play with music have received awards, including the Colorado Book Award and seven Colorado Authors League first place awards, the Willa Award for historical fiction, and most recently, first place from the Colorado Authors for her memoir, *Flying with El Condor*. Her greatest joy is teaching and her creative journey with other writers and artists.

KAY CROOK moved to Evergreen in 2003 from Dearborn, Michigan joining her son who had moved to Colorado several years earlier. She took early retirement from Ford in 2002 having worked in IT. She was introduced to Carolyn Campbell through classes at the Center for the Arts Evergreen. "My mother had senile dementia and I wanted to explore ways to exercise my mind, so I signed up for a memoir class." She now teaches IT and project management classes at the university level online and attempts to write poetry.

MARTHA DE ULIBARRI grew up in Louisiana and came to Colorado after graduating from college. She taught high school English for eight years, married, moved to Evergreen and took time off to have two daughters. Her marriage ended in divorce, and her sights were set on a career change. She received a Master's in Communication while using her writing skills in public relations positions. She now lives in Colorado Springs near her daughter and granddaughters and makes frequent visits to her other daughter and her family in Ireland.

LAURIE HILL GIBB came from common folks who scraped by in work of their hands. Her own work has been with children, with words, and fabric. Observing the nature of people and the nature of the earth are her main focus now. She hopes her legacy will settle around the theme of trying to make the world a better place on a planet that can sustain them.

BEV HANEY was born on a large farm in Manitoba, Canada. She moved to the U.S. in her early twenties and lived for many years in Minnesota. Bev and her husband Jim are retired and spend their summers in Colorado and winters in Mesa, Arizona. They both play bluegrass and country music and enjoy playing in jam sessions and entertaining in recreation centers and RV parks with a group called The Main Street Fiddlers. Bev has always loved to write but never had the courage to share her work with others until she started taking Carolyn Campbell's classes in Evergreen. Carolyn's encouragement and support inspired her to recall and put on paper her many childhood memories, some of which she has chosen to share in this anthology.

PATTY HOLLOW has enjoyed Carolyn's classes for years and although it was mostly poetry that she wrote, she did eventually branch out into personal short stories and a specific timeline to build her memoir. She is a retired makeup artist and she still keeps busy with her soup making and specialty cooking which was a business she started in Colorado called Zen Soup. She takes a storytelling class now and it is a new and fun venture for her.

MARCIA JONES has enjoyed a career of more than forty years, in corporate America with the exception of her first years as a high school English teacher. During the past few years she slowed her pace and found time to take poetry and memoir classes from Carolyn Campbell. While she considers herself more of a poet than a memoirist, she is pleased to participate in this book. She has lived in the Front Range foothills for more than thirty years.

CARL JURGENS lives in a stone and log cabin near Kittredge, Colorado with his wife Pat and their dog Zoe. Originally from Kentucky, he moved to Colorado in the late 70's. He has three sons and four grandchildren and a recent granddaughter-in-law. He participated in a memoir writing class with Carolyn Campbell. This is his first submission to be published.

PAT JURGENS moved "up the hill" to Evergreen in 2000, where she met and took her first writing class from Carolyn Campbell. She has participated in many of Carolyn's workshop get-aways in Grand Lake, Fairplay, Estes Park, and Georgetown. Pat has written articles for the *Mountain Connection* newspaper, *Serenity* magazine, *Outlook By the Bay* magazine, and the *JCHS Record.* She won a first-place award in the Jefferson County Historical Commission's magazine. She loves living in the mountains in an old cabin she shares with her husband Carl and dog Zoe. She is writing a historical novel set in the West in the early Twentieth Century.

SUSAN KERR is a former architect and park planner who loves the English language. Her professional writing career is in Biblical Studies, and she is a contributing writer, since 2013, to an international publisher of Bible commentary and curriculum: David C. Cook. She is currently working on an introductory overview to the Bible, *Seated at the Table, The Entire Bible in 17 Lessons.* Her other book in progress is a parallel journal of her life overlaid with her great-grandfather's. He was a Confederate soldier whose Civil War diary has led Susan to pursue him around Virginia and across time. Her memoir "The Meeting" in this anthology is taken from her book in progress.

NANCY LARNER took her first writing class from Carolyn Campbell in 2001 and a new world opened to her. Her poems have been published in several magazines and she was selected as Poet of the Month in *Poetica* magazine for her poem, "Reflections of Jewish Thought". She published a children's book, *A Mouse in the Rabbi's Study.* She is currently writing a memoir featuring seven generations of women in her family. Nancy is a talented artist who has exhibits in local and national galleries.

ELEANOR LANE LOWREY is a South Dakota girl. She was born to George and Eunice Lane on October 8, 1924, as an only and beloved child, and raised in a small town in the northeastern part of the state. She attended Macalaster College in St. Paul, MN where she met and married Jack Beltman Lowrey, M.D. After the fifth and last child went to school, she herself returned to school to continue her own education. She finished her B.A. and began her career as an educator. She started working for Jefferson County schools, earned her M.A. and Ed.D. (also at the University of Denver), and retired as Area Director for Special Education after twenty-five years of service to the District. She and Jack celebrated their 70th wedding anniversary in September 2015 and their family has grown to five children, sixteen grandchildren and twelve great-grandchildren. Jack died in January 2016. Eleanor continues to write to this day.

HILDEGARD MAAS comes from the Baltic Sea area in northern Germany. During WWII her home in Germany was occupied by the Nazi army. Her family was separated until united after the war and then went to America to start a new life in Minnesota. She and her husband and two sons moved to Chicago. Her husband died suddenly of a heart attack and she raised her sons and worked in Chicago for ten years. The death of her second husband left her once again on her own. She did art work at a community college and she retired from her computer job. She moved to Colorado to be near her oldest son.

PEGGY MARKHAM moved to Evergreen in 1987 and found her writing Muse here in the mountains. "It was Carolyn Campbell who launched me into writing creatively. I have met so many wonderful writers through her classes." She helped organize the local poetry chapter, Poets in the Pines. She has been honored to win awards for her poetry from state and national poetry societies and from the Denver Woman's Press Club. She finds inspiration for her writing from her family, her Southern heritage, the adventures she has had throughout her life, the places she has lived, and the support of her friends.

LAURA MEHMERT has been a working artist in watercolor, oil, sculpture, and quilting for over thirty years. In the mid-1990s she met Carolyn Campbell who has been instrumental as a teacher and mentor in Laura's journey as a writer and poet. Laura has published her own book of poetry. She is an acclaimed artist with local and national recognition. "Writing has been cathartic and healing for me."

LYNN MERGEN grew up in California and came to Colorado in 1963 as a student at Loretto Heights College. She earned a B.A., gained a love for the state, and met the love of her life, Don. They married in 1968 and as Don's job directed, they moved to many new, exciting places around the world. They have four children and seven grandchildren. Lynn and Don settled in Colorado in retirement. Lynn loves painting, writing, entertaining, spending time with her family and enjoying good laughs with friends.

ANITA NIELSEN is a native of Switzerland and resides with her husband in Conifer, Colorado. She has written articles for *Serenity* magazine and the *Mountain Connection* newspaper.

CAROLYN SEYMOUR is a working artist having earned a B.A. and M.A. Along with her husband, she worked as scientific liaison for the U.S. at the American Embassy in Ottawa, Canada and the UN in Paris, France. She has three children. She has been a teacher of printmaking and worked in William Hayter's Atelier 17 in Paris and Roger Barr's studio in Paris. She has exhibited her art nationally and received many art awards and prizes. Currently she is taking classes from Carolyn Campbell, studying writing techniques. She finds the same principles applied to producing two dimensional art also apply, somewhat, to written work.

MARY RYAN SIMONICH was supposed to be born at Ft. Bennington, Georgia; however, the brakes went out on her father's car in the Black Hills of South Dakota and instead she was born in

Rapid City. As an army brat, she lived in Georgia, Kansas, Germany, Utah, and Texas. By the time she graduated from high school, she had attended seventeen different schools. She graduated from Augustana in Sioux Falls. For one year she attended Creighton Law School. She is married and has two sons. She has lived in Evergreen for over forty years. Under the guidance of Carolyn Campbell, she is slowly learning the craft of writing, and in doing so, she is releasing her energy and her soul in her work.

BARBARA STERNBERG was born in England in 1923. She earned a B.A. in Sociology from the London School of Economics and an M.A. in Urban Sociology from the University of Denver. She married a Czech architect and planner, Eugene D. Sternberg in 1946. They had five children. In a long lifetime Barbara had a number of careers: university teacher, Jungian psychotherapist, author and poet. Barbara authored/co-authored four books including her last, *Anne Evans – a Pioneer in Colorado's Cultural Development: The Things That Last When Gold is Gone.* Barbara died July 15, 2016 just shy of her 93rd birthday. She was a longtime resident of Evergreen, Colorado.

KATE VAN WYHE was an only child in a funny, dysfunctional, big, Irish Catholic family. She has lived in Kansas City, Atlanta, Washington DC, Anaheim, Barstow (the less said there), Phoenix, and finally and happily, Denver, where the strange odyssey and her marriage ended. She earned a degree from Regis University in her 40's while raising her two children, remarried and has enjoyed his two children and three grandchildren. Kate worked for the Colorado Tourism Board and the Colorado Division of Housing before she retired and met Carolyn Campbell, who has been tirelessly trying to draw out her elusive writing abilities ever since.

CHARLOTTE VON BAYERN was born in Bavaria. She married a US military serviceman and came to America as a young bride, age twenty-one, in 1952. Currently she is working on a manuscript of her memoirs about growing up in Bavaria. She hopes her grandchildren and great-grandchildren will enjoy reading her stories of her life in "the Old Country". Taking writing classes from Carolyn Campbell has given her a discipline for her creative writing. She was an interior designer and has always enjoyed gathering items that remind her of her childhood.

SI WEIR is a retired hospital administrator and a current hospital chaplain in Denver. He is an ordained Deacon in the State of Colorado Episcopal Diocese. He and wife Eunice have three grown daughters and four grandchildren. Si is a volunteer with the Platte Valley Trolley and with the Trails and Rails joint venture between Amtrak and the National Park Service as a guide aboard the *California Zephyr.* A graduate of the University of Michigan he celebrates/suffers with the UM football team. He is "seasonally estranged" from his oldest daughter, Liz, an Ohio State University graduate and a rabid Buckeye fan.

LOUISE WHITESIDE earned a M.E. and M.S.W. and is a former teacher of English as a Second Language, and is a retired human resources specialist with the Department of the Army. As an independent consultant, she taught courses in time management and communication skills. Louise has written for *Good Old Days* magazine and is a regular contributor to *Outlook By the Bay* magazine.

CPSIA information can be obtained
at www.ICGtesting.com
Printed in the USA
FSOW02n0224011116
26830FS

9 781621 379133